OUTDOOR LEADERSHIP

It has often been said that leaders are born, not made. In *Outdoor Leadership*, John Graham's concise text describes the numerous elements, which are essential to the making of any leader.
—American Alpine Club

Anyone would benefit from this book, whether you are a leader of groups in the outdoors regularly, or if you are simply the one with more experience when hiking with your typical hiking partner. John Graham's 30+ years of experience make this book rich with common sense.
—*Signs for Northwest Trails*

Outdoor Leadership's discussion, advice, and techniques for learning and improving leadership skills will prove invaluable to anyone, hard-core mountaineer or not, in the outdoors or any other part of life. This book is so good I will strongly recommend it to all my staff and friends. A real gem.
—Gary Neptune, Owner, Neptune Mountaineering

OUTDOOR LEADERSHIP

Technique, Common Sense & Self-Confidence

by John Graham

THE
MOUNTAINEERS

Published by
The Mountaineers
1001 SW Klickitat Way, Suite 201
Seattle, WA 98134

First printing 1997, second printing 1997, third printing 1998, fourth printing 2002, fifth printing 2003, sixth printing 2004, seventh printing 2006, eighth printing 2007, ninth printing 2008, tenth printing 2009

Distributed in the United Kingdom by Cordee, www.cordee.co.uk

Manufactured in the United States of America

Editor: Mary Anne Stewart
Copyeditor: Deborah Kaufman
Cover design: Helen Cherullo
Book design: Alice C. Merrill

Cover photograph: *Hiker lends a helping hand in Telluride, Colorado.*
© Rick Ridgeway, Adventure Photo and Film

Library of Congress Cataloging-in-Publication Data
Graham, John, 1942–
    Outdoor leadership : technique, common sense & self-confidence / by John Graham
        p.   cm.
    ISBN 0-89886-502-6
    1. Recreation leadership.   2. Outdoor recreation.   I. Title.
    GV181.4.G73   1997
    790' .06'9—dc21   97-1379
                                                                    CIP

♻ Printed on recycled paper
ISBN: 978-0-89886-502-8

Contents

Preface

My first experience as a leader was not a success. Newly promoted to lead a patrol in Boy Scout Troop 99, I handled the first conflict I faced by socking Phil Adams and creating a general free-for-all on a trail near Mount Rainier. For that, I got benched.

I did improve. My leadership experiences have continued through four decades of outdoors adventures, from weekend trips with my family to the first direct ascent of the north wall of Mount McKinley.

It hasn't all been in the mountains. As a Foreign Service officer, I was in the middle of the revolution in Libya, then led a joint military/civilian team in one of the hottest areas of the war in Vietnam. During the Carter Administration, I guided a team of young diplomats that did groundbreaking work on certain third-world issues at the United Nations, including pressuring South Africa to end apartheid and opening a dialogue with Castro's Cuba.

Since 1982, I've been executive director of the Giraffe Project, a nonprofit organization that moves people to stick their necks out for the common good. The Project acts as a press agent for America's heroes, finding people already acting with courage and compassion to solve problems in their communities, or farther afield, then telling their stories in both national and local media, and in schools. Other people see and hear the stories of these "Giraffes" and are inspired to take on the challenges *they* see. The Project has now honored over 1000 Giraffes. Some work by themselves, but many of them have created and now lead organizations that carry out their work.

Everywhere I've been, from mountains in Peru to the United Nations to the communities touched by Giraffes, I've watched leaders, including myself, succeed—and I've watched us fail. The question has always been: what makes the difference? From weekend backpacking trips to international conflicts, what does it take to provide the leadership that saves situations—and sometimes lives?

In the early eighties I began putting my ideas on leadership and dealing with conflict into Giraffe Project speeches and workshops, which I've delivered to conferences, governments, corporations, labor unions, universities, and political and social action groups. Sponsored by international human rights groups, I've taken these ideas all over the world, working, for example, to heal conflicts in South Africa and Cambodia.

When I returned to my Washington State roots in 1985, I climbed with the Everett Mountaineers every weekend I could spare, helping to teach courses and leading trips. In 1993, The Mountaineers, concerned over some accidents and conflicts on club trips, asked me to tailor the Giraffe Project workshops into an outdoor leadership course for them. I quickly said yes. So much of what I'd learned about leadership had come from my own experiences on trails and mountains. The Everett course would bring what I knew full circle.

I led that course for over three years, in both Everett and Seattle, focusing on leadership situations and issues common to trips in the outdoors.

Most of this book comes from the materials developed for The Mountaineers' course. Nothing in it is untested theory. Many of the stories I've used come from my own life, which, for whatever reason, has been a succession of adventures, mishaps, near misses, and crises that have provided a rich environment for learning about leadership.

You'll quickly notice a major theme in this book—that good leadership is much more than the traditional hard-edged stuff such as planning, honing technical skills, making tough decisions, and dealing with conflicts. All of these elements are essential, but they are not enough.

What most often separates good leadership from bad, in my experience, is competence in the so-called soft-edged skills, such as developing trust, communicating with sensitivity, balancing intellect with intuition, and inspiring those you lead. Developing and using skills such as these tests your spirit as well as your mind, and challenges your ability to form positive relationships with those you lead.

Hard and *soft* get equal time in this book. Moreover, rather than setting them apart I've woven them together, since, in my experience, this is how they work in real life: intellect and intuition, head and heart—each overlapping with and reinforcing the other.

The ideas in this book have been circling in my head for years, growing and changing. And I'm still learning. Every leadership experience is an opportunity to learn something new and useful. It will be the same for you. There's plenty of opportunity for you to build on what is in this book, to carry the ball a little farther. Let the ideas you find here demand that of you. Let them demand that you test and refine them in your own way, serving not only what you do as an outdoors leader, but what you do with your life.

Chapter One

What Is Leadership?

Leadership is not a science to be picked up in one book or course, but an art to be learned over time. Good leaders sometimes tell people what to do, but leadership is not just giving directions—it's liberating people to do what is needed in the best possible way.

Like most mountaineers, I'm addicted to climbing stores. I pet the $500 sleeping bags. I play with the new hardware. I try on boots and parkas. But the new electronic stuff grabs me most of all—wrist altimeters, GPS devices, and the like. And of all that high-tech gear, for years it was an avalanche rescue beacon that I coveted the most.

An avalanche beacon, as you may know, is a small, single-frequency radio that transmits a steady beep when it's in *send* mode, and picks up beeps from transmitting beacons when it's turned to *receive*. The strength of the signal varies with the distance between the sending and receiving beacons. Carried on backcountry climbing or skiing trips, these gadgets have guided rescuers to many a climber or skier who has disappeared under five feet of wet snow. Since I was often out in Washington's Cascade Range—one of the most dangerous avalanche areas in the country—and since I had intentions of becoming an old man, I finally sprang for one.

––––––––

Using an avalanche beacon takes some training and practice, so I signed up that winter for a two-day course, held on the slopes of Mount Baker, near the Canadian border. For the first day and a half, the eight people in my training class practiced finding and "rescuing" beacons in gunny sacks buried in the snow. With our own beacons on *receive*, we each honed in on the signals from the buried sacks. We grew so accomplished that soon we could find a buried sack and dig it up in three minutes or less—which is a whole lot better than a Saint Bernard can do.

Then came our graduation test. For the first time in two days, the eight of us were told to work as a group. We were given some instruction on group rescues—for example, posting one person to watch for new slides. One of us, Tom, a crack telemark skier, was named leader. Tom was given no special instructions on what leaders of rescue teams were supposed to do. But he nodded gamely and away we went, directed to a nearby slope where the test would start.

Sure enough, no sooner had we got there than we found a "dazed" skier stumbling toward us, screaming that his partners had just been buried in a massive slide. We all dropped our packs, stuck in our earpieces, and prepared to break the course record for finding the buried sacks. Now all superstars with the equipment, we started crisscrossing the slope, with about the same level of coordination as kids on an Easter egg hunt.

Tom, unsure of how to deal with the growing chaos, made a few timid moves to impose order, but in vain. Since six of us headed to the side of the slope where the beeps were the loudest, one sack "died" because we were too late getting to the small ravine where it was buried. We lost more points because nobody remembered to stand lookout.

Driving home from the mountains that evening, I had plenty of time to think about the screwup. It wasn't lost on me that in a real crisis our poor coordination could have meant a lot more than a hypothermic gunny sack.

What had failed was not technical expertise, but leadership. Tom did the best he could, but like a lot of people who spend time in the outdoors, he'd focused his time and energy on learning technical, not leadership, skills. Suddenly anointed leader, he didn't know what was expected of him. The rest of us hadn't helped much as followers, charging off on our own before he even had a moment to collect his wits. And the training course we were taking had taught Tom nothing about leading. He was just supposed to know what to do.

The course was excellent in every respect but this one. It was also very typical of the outdoors trainings I've experienced in forty years of being around mountains and mountaineers.

It's not that outdoors organizations and people don't know that leadership is a major, often decisive, element in why some trips succeed and others fail. We've all had experiences that have ended either well or badly because of the leadership. Poorly trained leaders can produce bad outcomes of many kinds—a wet bivouac caused by poor trip planning; a minor accident that becomes a major problem because of rash decisions and poor communication; a negotiation that fails because no one has the skills to resolve a conflict. Some of us have been in jams in which leadership has meant the difference between life and death. Yet many, if not most, outdoors organizations will devote hours or days or years to teaching technical skills—but then assume that people will somehow pick up leadership skills by themselves.

Sure, some people do pick up leadership skills on their own and, given enough opportunity for trial and error, they do fine. But most do not. Especially in outdoors situations where bad leadership can have disastrous consequences, it's not wise to trust that competent leadership, with no formal training, will always emerge when needed.

But what is *leadership*? No two people seem to describe it the same way.

A good place to start the definition is to look at what people *expect* of leaders. Here is a list culled from hundreds of questionnaires collected at my outdoor leadership courses for The Mountaineers. Feel free to add to it.

People expect good leaders to:
- be good at planning and organizing;
- be self-confident;
- be technically competent, which for outdoor leaders includes competency in basic skills such as first aid, routefinding, and reading the weather;
- care for other people;
- make good decisions;
- be trustworthy;
- communicate well;
- inspire others to be at their best;
- build and maintain morale;
- be good teachers and coaches;
- be able to deal with difficult people and handle conflicts;
- be able to build and guide teams; and
- anticipate problems and deal with them proactively.

Expectations point the way to a definition, but there's more. Leadership is not a science to be picked up in one book or course, but an art to be learned over time. It's not simply a set of rules to be followed, but an ability to build relationships. It's not merely skills and techniques, but a subjective blend of personality and style. Leadership involves not only the body and the mind, but the spirit and character as well: good leaders have the intuition, compassion, common sense, and courage it takes to stand and lead.

Good leaders sometimes tell people what to do, but leadership is not just giving directions—it's liberating people to do what's needed in the best possible way. Good leaders don't depend on their position to give them authority; they depend on earning trust. They don't mandate good performance from those they lead; they inspire it.

From all of this, here's *my* definition: *Leadership is the capacity to move others toward goals shared with you, with a focus and competency they would not achieve on their own.*

I have no doubts that leadership can be taught, and that all the skills and qualities in the list above can be nurtured in anyone. Some of it, such as planning and organizing, is basic and straightforward. And some of it, such as instilling trust and using intuition, involves elements of spirit and character that can be both complex and sensitive. All of it is essential to good leadership, and all of it is covered in the chapters that follow.

Leadership issues are arranged in this book so that skills and insights in the earlier chapters are building blocks for later lessons. Chapters Two and Three, for example, deal with effective attitudes toward leading, and with trip planning and preparation. Chapters Four and Five discuss leadership styles and the particular opportunities and challenges for women in leadership roles. Chapter Six, on making decisions, focuses on the balance between intellect and intuition. Chapters Seven through Ten discuss caring, responsibility, communications, and courage. Chapter Eleven, on team building, introduces the key concept of vision, which carries through to Chapter Twelve, on resolving conflicts. Chapter Thirteen is about handling stress. Chapter Fourteen brings you in from the field to discuss leadership of organizations. Chapter Fifteen offers guidance on launching and leading political initiatives, such as those sparked by environmental concerns.

As a quick reference aid, each chapter ends with a "Learning to Lead" checklist of the key points just made.

The book's organization and style are meant to make the subject accessible. Leadership doesn't belong on a pedestal, reserved for the most talented few. It's a continuum of abilities, with all of us leaders-in-training.

Of course some people make better leaders than others, because of innate gifts, such as steady nerves and quick minds. But I'm convinced, from years of watching, that everyone can be a competent leader—even the shyest of wallflowers—at the level at which they need to lead. I'm not saying that anyone can be president of your organization, or get an expedition to the summit of Everest. And no organization should ever allow people to lead trips or events beyond their competencies. But every one of us can develop the leadership skills we need to meet the leadership challenges we deal with, right down to guiding a family beach walk in the rain.

It may not seem that family outings should require much in the way of formal leadership, and it's true that many of us go into the hills with our buddies without a designated leader. But the outdoors has a way of confounding expectations. It would be rare if you spent much time outdoors and never had to grapple with a significant leadership challenge caused, for example by an unexpectedly difficult group, or by a sudden emergency that demanded leadership skills.

These are the times when it's naive to expect that "someone" will step forward, and that competent leadership will "somehow" happen. If nothing else, consider leadership training to be a smart insurance policy.

Finally, while nearly all the examples and stories in this book focus on outdoors situations, the guidance in this book applies to leadership in *any* situation. You can use it to lead a company work team, to organize an event or campaign in your community, or to deal with your kids. Leadership issues crop up all over our lives; expect this book to affect more than your next hike in the hills.

What Is Leadership?

- ❑ **Leadership is a major, often decisive, element in why some trips succeed and others fail.**
- ❑ **Don't assume that competent leadership will always emerge when it's needed,** with no formal training.
- ❑ **Leadership is not a science to be picked up in one book or course, but an art to be learned over time.**
- ❑ **Leadership is not just giving directions**—it's liberating people to do what's needed in the best possible way.
- ❑ **Leadership is the capacity to move others toward goals shared with you, with a focus and a competency they would not achieve on their own.**
- ❑ **Everyone can be a competent leader**—even the shyest of wallflowers—at the level they need to lead.
- ❑ **Consider leadership training to be a smart insurance policy,** even if you're an outdoors person who never expects to join a club and have formal responsibilities for leadership.
- ❑ **Leadership training benefits everything we do**—not just our trips outdoors. Leadership issues crop up all over our lives.

Chapter Two

Attitudes

What you believe about leadership—your attitudes—will greatly influence the results you get as a leader. They'll not guarantee success—but they'll definitely improve your odds.

Certain attitudes, certain ways of looking at leadership, are essential. They make your role as leader easier and you more effective in it. Attitudes about caring, responsibility, and courage get their own chapters later in this book, but several others need discussion now. These are about self-image, self-reliance, listening to your heart, believing in people, valuing practice—and knowing that you're always in the right place at the right time.

See yourself as a leader—and know *why* you lead. How do you feel when others look to you to make decisions? How does the responsibility sit on your shoulders? For example:

It's your third time out as a trip leader and you're taking a bunch of beginners up an easy trail to Mosquito Lake. Your group is moving a little slower than you'd like, but the weather is fair and the wildflowers are out; you figure it'll be OK to cook dinner in the dark if you have to.

Suddenly, black clouds begin to pour over a ridge to the west, and within minutes a summer storm is bearing down on you. The first drops of rain are so big they kick up dust on the trail. Lightning forks behind the peaks above and the crash of thunder is so loud and near, you know the storm center will be on top of you in minutes.

You've just started up a long exposed ridge. If you continue up, the danger of being hit by lightning could be significant, and even if it isn't, the chance that someone will panic in a storm this big is very real. But if you head down into the forest below, you'll never make it to the lake before dark; you'll have to camp lower, and you're not sure of the water supply there.

Up until now there has been no need for anyone to "lead" on this easy, well-traveled trail. But now things have changed. This is Ben's first trip into the mountains. He is clearly getting more worried with each flash of lightning. "What'll we do?" he asks, directing his question at—you.

———————

This is no time to be shy about who's in charge. But neither is it time to throw your weight around; the members of your group are skittish enough as it is. What they need to feel, and what you need to call forth now, is a quiet, confident acceptance of your leadership role. You need to *see* yourself as a leader, functioning effectively as head of your group or team. It's that vision of yourself, that acceptance of your role, that squares your shoulders, settles your emotions, and prepares your mind and heart to lead.

A strong vision of yourself-as-leader doesn't come overnight. It grows and deepens as a product of training and experience. But you can speed that growth, and take on leadership roles more quickly and confidently, by exploring, and accepting at a gut level, the reasons *why* you lead.

Becoming a leader requires large amounts of time and effort. *Being* a leader also means taking on risk and responsibility. It's hard to sustain the commitment necessary to go through all this unless you have thought about, and acknowledged, the personal benefits of leading—and explicitly judged them worth the costs. Without that commitment, the picture you have of yourself as leader will be dim.

■

The most important aspect of leadership is having a reason for leading beyond investing in your own ego. It takes passion and genuine intention to be a good leader.

Always check your intention. Ask yourself why you lead. If your intentions have to do with ego and power, your team will pick up on this, and it probably won't work for you.

This is true for leadership anywhere. We started a private school in our community four years ago. In Canada, this was definitely not a popular idea and there was lots of opposition. But we persevered, because we knew the kids needed this—because we had intention.

—Sharon Wood, Adventure Dynamics, first North American woman to summit on Everest

■

Knowing and accepting the reasons why you lead not only helps sustain your commitment, it also sets the activity of leading firmly in the context of how you see yourself and what matters to you. This perspective makes the experience of leading more personally meaningful: you're leading because it fits with the priorities you've set for your life.

If leading makes sense to you at this deep level, you'll be more confident and comfortable in a leadership role. You'll also find it easier to summon the courage you need under stress, as described in Chapter Ten. Those around you will sense your confidence and courage, which will augment their own.

For these reasons, regularly reflect on why you lead, and why you take the time and accept the trouble that leading entails. I've seen too many people stay in leadership positions out of sheer inertia, because others expect it of them, or because it provides support for their egos. Motives such as these invariably produce poor leaders. And accepting leadership roles mindlessly is a prescription for burnout and failure. If it hasn't already, a time will surely come when the weather, an accident, or a conflict will test your conviction about wanting to lead. Especially in times like these, being confident of your motives will reinforce your picture of yourself as leader—and that will help you carry the day.

So ask yourself: why do you lead?

"Because I'm good at it and I like to do it" is a good start—but you can go deeper.

"I lead because I love the challenge of dealing with the unexpected. It heightens every adventure."

"I lead because it tests every part of me—and the sense of personal fulfillment is strong."

"I lead because I like people, and I'm challenged by bringing out the best in the people I'm with."

Another powerful motive is that leadership skills learned and practiced in the outdoors can be used every day of your life, and in every part of your life. The self-confidence that comes from leading doesn't disappear when you climb back into your car for the drive home. If you have the leadership skills and confidence to take a team up the side of a mountain, you can use those same skills to traverse all kinds of other slippery slopes at home, at work, or in your community.

Many outdoors people run businesses, for example, or they organize and coach sports teams, or they volunteer in the community in other ways. These sorts of activities demand leadership skills, such as organizing, setting goals, communicating, building and motivating teams, and resolving conflicts, that often are learned and practiced in the outdoors.

One of the greatest benefits of leadership is the opportunity it provides to be of service. It's extremely satisfying to be a coach and a role model out there, knowing that others are learning skills and traits that are changing their lives for the better—as your life has been changed by those who taught you. The opportunity to demonstrate, model, and teach the life skills that make up good leadership is a gift. It's a rare source of personal satisfaction and meaning.

Appreciate that leading can be lonely. Being friendly and accessible are valued leadership traits—but leading is not a popularity contest. There will be times, if you're doing your job, when you will have to say no or make other decisions that will disappoint or anger others. How clearly and confidently you see yourself as a leader, as discussed above, will strongly affect both the strength and grace with which you do this.

Similarly, don't over-rely on role models in learning to lead. While watching others is an essential part of leadership training—and there's certainly comfort in following in the steps of a more experienced person—there are limits. For one thing, not every role model you'll be exposed to will be doing it right. Learning the wrong moves letter-perfect can be hard to unlearn.

■

Leadership is not just passed on from the more experienced to the less experienced. There are too many people with a lot of experience who don't know what they're doing. Some people say that experience is the best teacher. To heck with that. I know people who've been making the same mistakes for forty years.
—Paul Petzoldt, founder of the National Outdoor Leadership School

■

But even if you're lucky enough to watch and learn from a series of impeccable models, there's still a good reason not to over-rely on them. Learning to lead is not like learning to do a stem turn, which good skiers all learn to do in pretty much the same way. Every good leader develops a personal leadership style dependent on personality, as described in Chapter Four. You can copycat only so far—then you have to meld basic principles into your own style and make it work for you.

Initially, you may feel lonely. But as you continue, you'll gain the confidence of knowing that your leadership is an expression of who *you* are, not an attempt to copy somebody else.

Value your heart as much as your head. Leadership training gets a lot more personal than learning hard-edged technical skills, as you'll quickly see as you continue in this book. You need to develop your abilities to sense others' feelings as well as your own, to balance rational and intuitive factors in making decisions, to have the "people skills" to resolve emotionally charged conflicts, and to be introspective.

Success in these areas demands that you have your heart in gear as much as your head. Trying to learn to be a leader by using your intellectual skills only—by sticking to the hard-edged, quantifiable stuff—is like owning a television set that tunes to only one channel: there's no way you can get the full range of information and insights you need.

Combining head *and* heart to lead means not accepting someone on your trip who is unqualified, but spending an hour on the phone getting him onto a trip that is appropriate and that he will enjoy. It means planning a flawless menu for a week in the wilderness for eleven people, and not forgetting candles for Gwen's birthday glop on Saturday. It means leading a twelve-hour scramble up a difficult peak, and watching the alpenglow *before* you sign the summit register, or plotting a perfect ski route across an alpine valley but taking a different path when you get there because your instincts tell you it's safer. It means training your team in rock climbing signals, and bothering to learn them in Spanish for the exchange student from Honduras. Using head and heart means making a terrific first ascent, then stopping to enjoy the wildflowers on the way down.

Making the head/heart connection not only provides information and insights that will make your trips safer and more likely to reach their goals, it also provides richer, fuller, and more personal experiences for everybody involved. As you become more adept at this, you'll be able to see for yourself how much better it works to have every part of you in play—and your confidence as a leader will grow.

Believe in people. One good way to measure the effectiveness of leaders is to measure their impact on those they lead. Good leaders often inspire others to perform at extraordinary levels. They don't do this by learning how to give great pep talks; rather, their capacity to inspire flows from a gut belief in the positive potential of people.

The confidence you have in others has an effect on how well they perform. For example:

You're on a climb where the most difficult part of a pitch is a diagonal traverse of a vertical ice wall. It's late afternoon, and a strong sun has been beating down for hours, softening the ice. As you watch from a safe perch above the traverse, you see the rest of your team ease across. Bill and Ed each have footholds break out from under them, but they recover—Ed just barely—and continue up. Now only Frank is left to go. Frank's a decent climber, but probably the weakest on your trip. He's also carrying thirty pounds on his back, and the sun has had another twenty minutes to further weaken the ice. The odds are that Frank will fall. You anchor the safety ropes securely; you'll stop him if he falls, but you'll have a difficult and dangerous time pulling him to safety.

You've done all the practical stuff. Now how do you hold this situation in your head?

Don't wait for Frank to fall. Instead, believe in his success. Shouting encouragement isn't enough. Every member of your team must create a mental picture of Frank planting his crampons, swinging his ice ax, and moving up and across that wall, almost as if every one of you were inside him, willing him forward. Frank will feel this, and it will affect how he moves, perhaps by exactly the few pounds of force or the few degrees of swing that separate a solid step from a fall. And that will be enough.

I'm not suggesting you throw people into situations in which they don't have the required experience, training, or skills. But by consciously believing in people and their potential, you can increase both their confidence and competence, especially in difficult and dangerous situations.

> A leader has to be the "rock." Sometimes on a trip you'll have negative and fearful people who drain energy from everyone. The leader has to operate in the opposite direction. The leader has to be not only a role model, but a source of energy and inspiration for the entire team.
> —Peter Whittaker, climber/guide, Summits Adventure Travel

Make practice a priority. Don't assume that, without practice, leadership skills will be there when you need them. Leaders who take the time and effort to keep their skills sharp are more likely to deal confidently with obstacles and conflicts, and to inspire confidence from those they lead.

Every once in a while I look out my office window at the fire station next door. Many times I see the firefighters rolling and unrolling hoses, coupling and uncoupling hydrants, placing ladders, and checking gear. Whenever I marvel at how much they practice, I remember the hundreds of times that I've practiced, for example, leading crevasse rescues. I'm confident that I could organize a pulley rescue system blindfolded, left-handed, and in a howling blizzard.

The truth is, in my decades of climbing on glaciers, I've only had to do a real crevasse rescue two or three times. Each of those times, the fallen climber was conscious and managed to climb out on his own; all the rest of us had to do was secure his rope. So I've never had to organize and use a pulley rescue system in an actual fall. The fact that I know how to do it if I have to, however, adds a whole lot to my confidence in leading groups across dangerous ice.

Part of the neverending process of leadership training is practicing complex but repeatable techniques such as crevasse rescues, or fixing your position in the outdoors by using a compass and map. Books can help you update these skills. Courses and refresher courses given by local outdoors organizations can help you keep them sharp.

Another part of leadership training is mastering processes—such as making decisions or dealing with conflicts—that demand different moves every time. There are far fewer books and courses available here to help you improve your skills. Get feedback from the people you lead. Keep notes of what does, and doesn't, work. Share experiences and solicit advice from other leaders, especially those who've been at it longer than you have.

The skills and confidence you gain in mastering both techniques and processes are cumulative. And nobody's perfect. If you're not making some mistakes, then it's unlikely that you're pushing the edges of your growth as a leader hard enough. Mistakes are an essential part of that growth. The only way to really fail is not to learn from them.

Take time to evaluate your performance after every trip. Note what worked, especially if you were trying it for the first time. And look hard at what didn't work. If you don't fully understand what went wrong, then do research and/or talk to more experienced leaders until you do. Don't stop until you're satisfied that you can do better next time.

Know that, as a leader, you're always in the right place at the right time. It's inevitable that some leadership challenges will come upon you unexpectedly, while others will suddenly become far more difficult than you bargained for. When that happens, don't waste time wondering why—it's not a mistake that you're there.

At the Giraffe Project, we interview many people who take on significant and dangerous leadership challenges, such as running drug dealers out of their neighborhoods or taking on a major institution over problems of corruption or pollution. When we ask these people why they take on such daunting tasks, their most common response is a shrug of the shoulders. The challenge was right in front of them, they say, nobody else was stepping up—what else were they supposed to do?

That response makes a lot of sense. If a crisis suddenly develops in front of you and you're thrust into a leadership role, or if the leadership situation you're in suddenly grows difficult, there's no sense wishing you were someplace else. You're trained as a leader—who better than you to deal with whatever needs to be done?

Emergencies stretch good leaders but rarely break them. My belief is that you would not be the one challenged if you were not up to the task. If you trust that the inner reserves you need will be there, you'll raise the odds considerably that they will be.

Then do what you have to do.

Attitudes

☐ **See yourself as a leader—and know *why* you lead**. This makes the experience of leading more personally meaningful, which makes you more confident and comfortable in that role. As you list your own reasons, consider the following.

- *Leadership skills, and the self-confidence that comes from leading, affect every part of your life.*
- *Teaching and modeling leadership skills provide rare opportunities to be of service.*

☐ **Appreciate that leading can be lonely**. There will be times when you'll have to make unpopular decisions. How clearly and confidently you see yourself as a leader will strongly affect both the strength and grace with which you do this.

Don't over-rely on role models. You can copy-cat only so far—then you have to meld basic principles into your own style, and make it work for you.

☐ **Value your heart as much as your head**. Develop your abilities to sense others' feelings as well as your own, to balance rational and intuitive factors in making decisions, to resolve emotionally charged conflicts, and to be introspective.

☐ **Believe in people**. The confidence you have in others has an effect on how well they do.

☐ **Make practice a priority**. Don't assume that, without practice, leadership skills will be there when you need them. Learn from your mistakes.

☐ **Know that, as a leader, you're always in the right place at the right time**. If you're suddenly thrust into a leadership role, or if that role suddenly intensifies, don't waste time wondering why this is happening to you.

Chapter Three

Getting Ready

There may be more interesting and challenging aspects of leading in the outdoors than trip preparation. But no aspect of leading counts for more. A well-organized, well-prepared, and well-informed group will not only be more likely to reach its goals and avoid accidents, it's also far more likely to have a good time.

Getting ready to lead an outdoors trip starts with you: with your body, your technical skills, and your equipment. After you've made a plan, get the help and develop the management tools you need to carry it out. Establish requirements for people wanting to come, then assess their qualifications. When you have your group, use preliminary calls not only to convey information but also to start building personal relationships with people you don't know. Before you step into the woods, make sure you're aware of any special concerns, such as medical conditions. Then—although you've double-checked everything—be ready for the unexpected.

Get yourself ready first. Getting ready to lead an outdoors trip demands organizational skills, hard work, and a lot of common sense. The first step is to make sure that your own body and technical skills are ready. Part of this is learning to realistically and continually assess your own performance, and to respect personal limits.

Keep your body in shape. While leadership is about far more than physical strength and endurance, no outdoors leader—whether large or small of stature—can afford to be out of shape. Run, work out at a gym, do any special exercises, such as hand and ankle strengtheners, needed for your particular sport. Do what you need to do to maintain enough physical strength and endurance to handle the physical challenges of any trip you're on.

This does not mean—especially if you're a veteran and some of the people on the trips you lead are half your age—that you have to be the most physically fit member of the group because you're the leader. A good rule of thumb is that you should have at least average endurance in any group you're leading; you don't have to be at the fore of every charge to the top of the hill. But while you don't have to be the very strongest, it's not OK if the entire team has to keep waiting for you to get your sweating, panting body up there. Carry a share of group gear appropriate to your size, but if some strapping teenager wants to carry all the tents by himself—hey, we should all be so lucky.

Make sure your technical competence is up to what the trip requires. If you're on a trip requiring special technical competence, such as climbing steep rock or ice, or kayaking a dangerous stretch of rapids, you must be able to do that. As trip leader, however, you need not be the most technically proficient member of the team. And it's perfectly OK to ask someone more technically competent to lead a difficult pitch or section of the trip. Sometimes it might be irresponsible if you *didn't* ask.

Expedition mountaineering is a good case in point. Effective leadership for such a large, complex, and often dangerous undertaking requires a rare array of skills and experience, much rarer than sheer physical competence. A crack young climber might make the strongest dash for the summit, but it's the trip leader, the one with some gray hair back at high camp, who's most responsible for the team's success.

As a general rule, don't *lead* trips you know will push you to the limit of your personal strength or technical competence. It's fine to push yourself to the edge if you don't have leadership responsibilities—that's how you get better. But as trip leader, your role is bigger than leading all the hard technical sections yourself. Unless there's no choice, you should not be the one who risks getting exhausted or overextended on some all-or-nothing move. Nor should the biggest challenge for your group suddenly become how to get its leader up (or off) the cliff.

Of course, where competence most often counts is with basic skills such as orienteering, first aid, weather savvy, loading packs, tying knots, setting a pace, staying warm and dry, pitching tents, finding water, and cooking in the outdoors. Before every trip, review the skills you know could be tested on that trip—including any basic ones you sense might be getting rusty. You may want to do this off by yourself—no reason why a tenderfoot has to watch you practicing a basic knot!

Realistically and continually assess your own performance, and respect personal limits. One of the most difficult aspects of leadership is knowing and respecting your own limits of strength and technical skill. Taking on challenges above your level of competence is bad enough when you're by yourself. It can be a multiple disaster if you're leading others.

Self-assessments aren't easy.

A couple of years ago I found myself halfway up a difficult rock face in the Cascades. The rock was solid, I was with Tom and Don, my favorite climbing buddies, and the sky was blue. So why wasn't I having any fun? I was breathing hard, my knuckles were bloody, and my knees were knocking. It didn't take much introspection to realize I was struggling up moves that, a few years earlier, I used to make with precision and grace. And that, for one of the few times in my life in the outdoors, I was genuinely afraid of falling. No wonder I wasn't enjoying my day! The balance and flexibility that had gotten me up so many other climbs weren't what they had been—and no amount of hours in the gym would bring them back.

It was an interesting moment, standing on a narrow belay ledge 2,000 feet above the valley floor. "Your turn to lead," said Tom, pointing up at a wall that looked as smooth as a pane of glass. I looked up, then told my friends it would be better if I could follow them. They joked and made all the rude remarks you'd expect from good friends, but the truth is, that moment was a very big deal for me. I had to face the fact that my balance and agility were no longer good enough to lead rock and ice pitches at that level of difficulty.

There is just as much a need for honest assessment at the other end of the age spectrum. Young leaders sometimes don't know when their skill level is insufficient for a difficult climb or task. Bravado sounds great around the campfire the night before the climb, but it's no fun the next day when somebody gets hurt or lost because a young leader's ambition was greater than his skills.

Keep your equipment ready to go. Many outdoors activities seem to call for new skills and new techniques almost every season, much of it driven by the invention of new equipment. This pace of innovation affects the skills you need. Staying warm and dry today is easy compared to what it was before Gore-Tex and artificial down. Sound compass and map skills will never go out of style—but satellite global positioning systems are getting smaller and cheaper every year. And camp cookery used to be far more of a challenge and an art before freeze-dried and other inventive trail foods came on the market.

But don't put all your eggs into the technology basket—human outdoors skills will never go out of date, especially for leaders. This is, in part, because the outdoors is a physically punishing environment, and sensitive gear can break and fail. But the real argument is that many functions in the outdoors are—happily—still out of reach of machines. It's fine if you want to use some satellite to tell you where you are on a mountain, but that satellite will not tell you how to build a fire in the rain, load a pack, avoid an avalanche slope, or spot a crevasse before you or some member of your team falls into it.

Especially if you lead or intend to lead: master basic outdoors skills and equipment first. Do this not only because someday you may be caught out without your high-tech gear. Do it also for the quiet inner confidence that comes from knowing that you know ten extra ways to stay warm and dry, that you can find some food and water anywhere, lead your team down with only a compass and map, and read the weather in the sky.

Keeping your equipment ready and knowing how to use it counts for anyone heading into the outdoors; it's *imperative* for leaders, who may get so caught up in other peoples' gear problems in difficult situations that they have neither time nor opportunity to deal effectively with their own. Your stuff *must* be there for you, ready to go when you need it, and you must be able to use it in the dark, in the rain, with half your team shouting for you to help them.

Discipline yourself to think ahead about your gear. Clean, dry, oil, and repair your equipment immediately after one trip ends—not the night before the next one begins. Routinely check batteries and light bulbs. Clean your boots, and, if they are leather, smear on a fresh coat of grease that can work itself in while they are waiting in the closet for the next trip. Reseal that leaky seam in your tent or parka. Patch that little hole in your bivvy sack before it becomes a big hole in some storm at 6,000 feet.

Check yourself out on any new pieces of gear. Some—such as avalanche rescue beacons—may require special instruction or courses. If you're checking out gear at home, however, make the tests realistic. Don't practice setting up that new tent in your living room—take it out in the backyard and do it in the dark a couple of times.

Think of all your personal preparations as being like those described in the safety videos on airplanes, instructing you to put on your own oxygen mask before helping others. As leader, you may very well have your hands full on the trip with other peoples' physical problems, equipment failures, or lack of skill. You probably won't have time to deal with any problems of your own—which is why you need to take care of them in advance.

Get organized. Winging it is fine—if you really like to get lost, eat uncooked Top Ramen because you forgot the fuel for the stove, and listen to everybody's complaints about your trip planning. But if you're like the rest of us who don't enjoy that kind of misery, spend the necessary time and energy to competently plan and organize your trip.

Research the trip. Check the relevant guidebooks and websites. Obtain the necessary maps. Listen to the weather reports. Call ranger stations to find out about road closures and other special circumstances, such as avalanche conditions. Ask questions of those who have gone before.

Make a plan—but don't set it in concrete. Block out the time needed. Plot the route. Determine the group and personal equipment needed. Establish meeting times and transportation requirements. Leave the planning process open and flexible so you can take into account new circumstances and information.

Get help if you need it. Determine what help you may need, and get it. If the trip is large, such as a basic training course, you'll need assistant leaders and other helpers.

Don't simply put out a call for help and accept anybody who answers. Carefully assess the functions that have to be filled and the competencies needed to fill them. Then spend enough time and effort to get the right people to take on the jobs you've defined. Make sure your people are informed and trained. This extra prep work pays rich dividends when your trip/event is in full swing and you know you can depend on *all* your team members to do their jobs.

Develop and use the management tools you need to keep track of details— cars, equipment, food, maps, guides, weather and avalanche reports. I know mountaineers who swear that all they ever need are 3 x 5 cards to plan anything from their kids' birthday parties to expeditions to the Karakoram. On the other hand, I know people who probably consider taking their laptops into the mountains.

The larger the event or trip, the more comprehensive and sophisticated your management tools need to be. I rely on a computer to help me keep track of trip planning chores. I use as many lists as are necessary: I might keep track of cars and other transportation requirements on one, for example, and group members' names, phone numbers, and other key information on another. Equipment always tends to present a major organizational challenge, so I have one whole list that deals with my personal gear alone. I understand that this might be overkill for you, but, as an example, here's how my personal equipment list works.

First, I enter every piece of outdoors gear I own, with a code that identifies where that item is stored. In the example below, GS means the gear storage room in my house, B, the basement, and BC, the bedroom closet. Then I identify every conceivable kind of trip I might lead. Finally, I create a grid, with items of equipment listed vertically and types of trips horizontally. If a piece of equipment is essential to a particular kind of trip, I put an E in that grid square. If it's optional, I enter O, and if it's not needed, I leave the square blank. When I'm planning for a trip, all I need to do is select the correct column and look for all the Es and Os.

So one section of my overall chart looks like this:

PERSONAL EQUIPMENT LOCATOR

ITEM	LOCATION	Family backpack	Rock climb *(day trip)*	Ice climb *(weekend)*
heavy sleeping bag	GS			E
light sleeping bag	GS	E		
Thermarest pad	GS	E		E
bivvy sac	GS	E	O	E
2-person tent	GS			E
4-person tent	B	E		O
stove	GS	E		E
fuel bottle	GS	E		E
fuel bottle #2	GS	O		O
eating gear	GS	E		E
large water bottle	GS	E	E	E
belt canteen	GS	E	E	E
cook kit	GS	E		E
ice ax	GS			E
ice tool	GS			E
crevasse rescue gear	GS			E
crampons	GS			E
heavy wool shirt	BC			E
light wool shirt	BC	E	E	O
wool pants	GS			E
light pants	BC	E	E	
polypro undershirt	BC	E	E	E
polypro long johns	BC	E		E
heavy socks	GS			E
light socks	BC	E	E	E
parka	GS	E	E	E
9 mm rope	GS		E	E
10.5 mm rope	GS		E	E
slings	GS		E	E
hard hat	GS		E	E
harness	GS		E	E

If your living setup allows, keep all or most of what you're likely to need for your outdoors trips in one place. Keep everything clean, visible, and ready to go. Store small, similar items together in Ziploc bags and hang the bags from clamps along a wall. One bag, for example, might be your repair kit with such items as wire, duct tape, Thermarest and Gore-Tex patches, and a crampon wrench. Another, your crevasse rescue kit, might contain the pretied loops of rope or sling material needed for that purpose. Other Ziploc bags might be your kits for camp cleanup and toiletries. The idea is never to have to scramble looking for little things late Friday night, when the phone is incessantly ringing with trip members calling with last minute questions.

With all you have to think about as leader, you're doing yourself a favor by making trip planning and organization as trouble-free as possible. Whether or not you use a computer, develop whatever tools work for you to help you organize your own gear. Use similar tools to keep track of, for example, personnel, transportation, and group equipment.

Because of the high stress and time urgency of search and rescue work, we must use prepared plans and checklists. In an emergency, we can quickly run our fingers down the relevant lists and make sure we have or are doing everything. It's surprising how often we come up with something crucial, for example, a key piece of equipment, that might have been forgotten if it weren't for those lists.

You have to carefully think through what you're going to need on any outdoors trip, because you can't take it all. In my personal pack, for example, I don't carry a big first aid kit, since any person I treat usually will soon be in a hospital. I'm also big on focusing on multiuse items. Cardboard splints are a great example. You can use them to pad your pack, to sit on in the snow, or to sleep on when on a bivouac. And they're great for starting fires!

Good preparation isn't only about making sure you have all the stuff you need. You also need to make sure that the stuff is in the right place, especially if you have to move fast. Anything I know I'll need early and often—such as tape—I always put in the lid of my pack. Anything else that might be essential but whose use is seldom urgent—such as painkillers—can go down in the bottom.

—Tim Auger, Public Safety Specialist, Search and Rescue, Banff National Park

---

Establish requirements and assess qualifications for people asking to come on the trip. Make sure that everyone understands the level of difficulty of the trip and the anticipated pace, and has the equipment and skills required. If your trip demands technical skills, develop a checklist of questions to ask of people you don't know, patterned after the checklists now demanded of climbers in many national parks. What is the applicant's history in this sport over the last five years, including levels of difficulty and results? What is their level of skills training and which courses have they taken, and from whom? Also ask about their present physical shape, especially if they have not been out too often lately. Do they run or go to a gym or work out at home?

Of course asking all these questions of newcomers can be much more trouble than making blind assumptions about competence and hoping for the best. Resist the temptation to make such assumptions, or to accommodate earnest people who you suspect are not up to the trip you're about to lead. If you're not satisfied that someone is adequately prepared, it's much wiser to tell them they can't come than endanger them or detract from the experience of others.

You can do this with grace. Explain your reasons carefully. Suggest other trips that might be more suitable and provide phone numbers of other leaders. Describe any available skills-building courses and provide information about how to sign up for them. Make it clear that you'll welcome them on future trips once the qualifications have been satisfied.

Use preliminary calls not only to convey needed information, but to build relationships. In addition to level of difficulty, pace, and required skills, make sure the people coming on your trip have all other basic, necessary information, such as where to meet, and at least general knowledge of what they can expect in terms of weather and route. Add any other information specific to that trip; remind everyone signing up for a hot August hike, for example, that they will need two water bottles, not one. Consider mailing out a list of required and suggested equipment, especially if you have a lot of beginners along.

You can also use these calls as a way of breaking the ice with people you don't know or don't know well. Interpersonal dynamics are often what separates a good from a bad trip. As leader, you want to know what you have to deal with. If you can't meet in advance those team members you don't yet know, then at least make an introductory phone call.

Start building the friendly, trusting relationships that will contribute to the success of the trip—and that could become crucial if a crisis develops. You might do this by offering personal observations and thoughts about the trip that you think will be useful to them. Tell the camera buff to bring her camera; the wildflowers should be gorgeous. Assure the beginner for the third time that the skills he recently learned in a cross-country ski course will be adequate for this trip. Ask everyone to share their expectations, concerns, and questions. Tell each member who else is coming—both by way of introduction and to encourage doubling up on equipment such as tents and stoves.

Determine special concerns. Make sure you know of any team member's special concerns or requirements, such as medical conditions. It's not uncommon to have someone along who must take insulin or another medicine while on the trip. Other people might have heart conditions, asthma, epilepsy, or be allergic to bee stings. In addition to relying on your own first-aid training, ask any trip member who reports a special condition what they want you to do for them in case of an attack. You need to know where to find their medicine and what dosage to give, in case that person should be unable to self-administer the medicine.

Medical conditions factor in more often than you might think. Not long ago a fellow I was with on a trip suddenly had a mild epileptic seizure as the two of us were gingerly traversing a steep, rocky slope. I managed to get him to safety, but it was not a fun experience. Had I known of his condition I would never have taken him on terrain that rough. Sure, he should have told me in advance, but the experience taught me a lesson: I will never again fail to ask people I don't know about medical conditions.

Double-check key factors, then check them again. A sobering aspect of outdoors trips is that once you've forgotten some key element, it's next to impossible to replace it on the trail. While it's fine to try to keep trip planning informal, don't let this informality turn into sloppy organization or management. Make a confirming phone call or send an email to each team member one or two days before the trip. Share the latest reports on weather or snow conditions. Give any reminders about necessary trip equipment. Confirm key group equipment, such as ropes, hardware, tents, stoves, and gas.

If you're planning to use any club equipment, check its condition well in advance. If somebody in the club stowed a tent wet last month and it's mildewed, better to find out about it now than later.

Do a final check of group and personal equipment at the trailhead—no matter how eager your group is to plunge into the woods.

Expect the unexpected. Don't wait until problems or crises find you. Focus on preventing problems rather than reacting to them. Yes, you've done a superb job of planning. Yes, you've talked to all your team members and they are as ready as they can be. Yes, you've double- and triple-checked every detail. Now, three days later and miles from the cars, who could have guessed that a sudden forest fire would cut you off from an essential trail and that going the long way around to avoid the fire will take an entire extra day?

Did you bring enough food and cooking gas to stretch? Did you bring the larger scale map showing your new route? Did you advise Bob not to schedule his business meeting for the morning after you were due back because—well, because you never know?

Getting Ready

❑ **Get yourself ready first**—you may have your hands full with other peoples' problems once you're on the trail.

- *Keep your body in shape.* Require at least average endurance among members of any team you lead, and adequate physical strength for that trip.
- *Make sure your technical competence is up to what the trip requires,* but remember you need not be the most technically competent member of the team. Don't lead trips that you know will push you to the limit of your strength or skill.
- *Realistically and continually assess your own performance, and respect personal limits.*

❑ **Keep your equipment ready to go,** and continually review your competence with it.

❑ **Get organized.**

- *Research the trip.*
- *Make a plan—but leave it open and flexible.*
- *Get help if you need it.*
- *Develop and use the personal management tools you need to keep track of details*—cars, equipment, food, maps, guides, and more.

❑ **Establish requirements and assess qualifications of people asking to come on the trip.** Don't hesitate to say no if you have to.

❑ **Use preliminary calls not only to convey needed information, but to build relationships.**

❑ **Determine special concerns, such as medical conditions.**

❑ **Double-check key factors, then check them again.**

❑ **Expect the unexpected.**

Chapter Four

Leadership Style

Identifying your own leadership style lets you maximize its strengths and compensate for any weaknesses. Whatever your style, it must be authentic. If the people following you know that "what they see is what they get," they will feel more comfortable with, and trusting of, you as leader.

Leadership is more than a set of rules and learned skills—it's an art, one in which your individual personality plays a major role. It's this imprint of personality onto your skills and experience that constitutes your leadership *style*.

Many styles can work. There are as many different styles of leadership as there are leaders—which is one reason the subject of leadership can be so complex. Some leaders communicate a decision in a sentence, while others take a paragraph. Some smile, some don't. Some seem to be in constant motion, while others move more deliberately.

Sally, for example, is a woman of few words. She knows that her quiet competence can inspire great confidence from those she leads. She's also aware of how others might misinterpret her quietness, and has learned to compensate. For example, right at the trailhead, she might remark jokingly about her nature: "I'm not dead out there, folks, just quiet."

Jerry, on the other hand, is always the life of the party. But he knows that leadership is serious business and watches his banter, especially around people he doesn't know. He doesn't ignore his responsibilities nor pull stunts that will have people doubting his competence—but he's learned that his sense of humor can be a powerful tool for defusing conflicts and relaxing others in tense situations.

Make use of your style. The more aware you are of your natural leadership style, the better you'll be able to make use of its advantages, turn possible disadvantages into strengths, and head off any misinterpretations.

> Humor is a big plus—especially being able and willing to laugh at yourself. Even the best leader will make mistakes. Don't set yourself up to fall harder by being grim about it. Humor also helps others on your trips know that you're accessible, and will help you build stronger relationships with your team.
> —Peter Whittaker, climber/guide, Summits Adventure Travel

Let's say that you were born with a relentless passion for details. You remember the last time you oiled your lawnmower. You failed to balance your checkbook only once, and that was in 1992, the week you got married.

Your leadership style reflects this very thorough and tidy personality. There are plusses and minuses to this, and you need to be aware of both.

You need to know, for example, that the people in your groups really appreciate your matchless ability to plan a trip—despite their good-natured ribbing about your careful nature. No one on your trips ever has to worry about tents without tent poles, or missing maps or canoe paddles. At the same time, however, you need to remember that your insistence on quadruple checking *can* annoy people and, in extreme cases, undermine your relationships with them. To make best use of your style, you need to accurately estimate where to draw the line between competent planning and overkill. And, like Sally, you may want to cut loose your sense of humor and do some good-natured ribbing of your own.

Your style must be you. Don't ever try to lead by being someone you're not. Your leadership style must be authentic; it must reflect who you are, with all the plusses and minuses that may entail. If your style is truly your own, it will make you and your leadership more credible, both to others and to yourself. If people following you know that "what they see is what they get," they will feel more comfortable with you and trusting of you as leader. This is a vital quality, especially if a problem or crisis arises on the trail.

If your style isn't authentic, group members will quickly sense the confusion and insecurity behind the faking, and you'll have a much harder time gaining their trust and cooperation. Never try to change your personality to fit someone else's image of what a leader should be. And while giving all due credit to the role models that helped shape your leadership skills, be aware that you're not them. At some point, you must focus on how your own personality affects your leadership, and acknowledge and develop your own leadership style.

The temptation to fake a leadership style is strongest for new leaders, whose self-confidence is still building. If you're new to leading, remember: no one expects you to be a grizzled veteran. Do your best, and your group will support you. Try to act like the old pro you're not, and you'll really worry people. They won't even trust you to do what you *are* good at, and that will make your job a lot more difficult.

■

In the old days, a lot of European climbers said that American climbing was too "democratic" and that's why a lot of summits weren't reached. They advocated a much more dictatorial approach to leadership.

This can go too far. I think it's best to give people some opportunity to see what you see and to help make the tough decisions. If I'm leading a group on a mountain and I can see from the weather that there's no way we should go on, I don't just make that announcement. I call for a break. Instead of saying right off, "We're going back," however, I'll wait a few minutes. People cool off from the hard work and sense the conditions better. They have a chance to look up at the weather ahead, to think about the time, and to puzzle things through for themselves. Then I ask people what they think. Often, they'll be the ones to suggest we go back. If they don't do that, then I've got no choice but to be the "dictator" and turn the group around, but at least I tried.

—Lou Whittaker, climber/guide, President of Rainier Mountaineering Inc. and author of *Lou Whittaker: Memoirs of a Mountain Guide*

■

So what is your leadership style? If you've never thought about it, don't start by trying to analyze it with your mind. The answers you're seeking are much too intuitive and nonrational for that. Instead, try the following metaphor exercise with someone who knows you well. It will help you coax out insights that will be more reflective and accurate than those your intellect alone can provide.

The Metaphor Exercise. Close your eyes and see yourself in whatever leadership roles you already play—in the outdoors or at home, at work or in the community. Then have a friend start by asking you, "When you're leading—if you were an animal, what would you be?" Answer with the first image that pops into your mind: "When I'm leading, I'm a sheepdog." "I'm an old stag." "I'm a chimp." After you've answered, turn on your intellect to see if you can find reasons for the match your intuition just sensed. For example, "When I lead I'm a sheepdog because I'm always circling the flock." "I'm an old stag—I'm quiet, stern, and aloof." "I'm a chimpanzee who keeps things light and playful."

Have your friend repeat the same question using other metaphors, such as food, musical instruments, and cars. Your answers may be very enlightening: "When I'm leading, I'm a Volvo, because I'm really solid." "I'm a combo pizza—I tend to use all kinds of styles, depending on the situation." "I'm a trumpet—lots of noise and everybody knows exactly what I want."

Does your friend agree with your assessments? Do you see your style as eagle, for example, but your friend thinks donkey? Do you envision electric guitar, but your friend thinks string quartet?

This exercise is fun, but it's not a game. The discussions that inevitably follow can get you to think hard about your leadership style, as perceived by you and others. These insights are invaluable as you test and refine your style, and deepen your experience as a leader.

Never-ever styles. Of course, there are some "never-evers" in leadership style—behaviors that don't work and should never be tried, no matter how authentic they might be. For example, being insulting, sarcastic, sexist, or manipulative is inexcusable. Outdoors trips are not forced marches and you're not a drill sergeant.

There are times, as we will see below, when it's appropriate and necessary to be an authoritarian leader—but this can be done with respect and caring. Don't let anyone tell you that insensitive, bullying behavior, no matter what the circumstances, is "just my style." This sort of behavior masks a lack of self-confidence that will lead to serious mistakes in judgment.

Henry Kissinger, for whom I once worked, led the State Department by fear and intimidation. He bullied his staff unmercifully and ran through personal secretaries at a rapid rate—it was not uncommon to see one running in tears out of his office. Respected for his intelligence, he was hated for his leadership style. He never understood why so few of us were loyal to him. Nobody trusts a bully.

Flexibility in style—the Pucker Factor. Leadership styles need to be not only authentic and respectful but flexible enough to respond effectively to fast-changing situations. Depending on those situations, anyone's leadership style should be able to range from rigidly authoritarian to completely consensual.

■

I tell all the leaders who guide for me never to cluster with each other on the breaks, but to mix in with all the other team members. A leader has to know, however, when it's not appropriate to be "one of the gang." It's one thing to put aside the leadership role and join in the fun around the campfire, but you also have to know when to turn up the heat, particularly if there's a safety concern.

—Peter Whittaker, climber/guide, Summits Adventure Travel

■

If you see an absentminded person on your trip about to step onto a loose rock and cause a dangerous fall, you grab the person and pull him out of harm's way. This is an extremely authoritarian and entirely appropriate leadership response under the circumstances.

But when four buddies go off on a fishing trip, the decisions to be made (say, when to stop for lunch) are so routine that the most appropriate leadership is informal and consensual—so much so that it's hard to call it leadership at all.

These two examples are the extreme ends of a scale called the Pucker Factor, from an old Army term describing the degree of body tension generated by varying levels of stress. In this book, Pucker Factor is a measure of how authoritarian and controlling leadership needs to be in a specific situation.

According to the Pucker Factor, as the gravity of a situation increases—and/or as the competency of a group to handle that situation decreases—the leadership style must become more authoritarian. Under these conditions, the time needed to reach consensus is often not available and even if it were, consensus leadership is often poorly suited to meet the challenges of a demanding crisis (see below).

The Pucker Factor depends not only on the gravity of the situation and the competency of the group but also on the *relationship* between the two. Those who like math can see this relationship as an equation: $P=G/C$, where P is the Pucker Factor, G is the gravity of the situation, and C is the competence of those being led.

For example, when you see your team member about to step on that unstable rock, the Pucker Factor is extreme and the leadership should be authoritarian—not only because the gravity of the situation is high, but also because the person is oblivious to the danger and therefore his competence to save himself is low.

With the fishing buddies, the situation is so safe that even modest competence is enough to keep the Pucker Factor low—and the appropriate leadership, informal consensus.

Because the Pucker Factor is a relationship, it might actually remain low in a dangerous situation, provided the group competence is high enough.

In the summer of 1963, I was part of a seven-man team from the Harvard Mountaineering Club that put up the first direct ascent of Mount McKinley's north wall. The climb was reasonably difficult and quite dangerous; it took us more than a month to inch up that wall. The situation was sometimes fairly grave, but the seven of us planned and climbed competently enough, and worked so well together as a team, that our Pucker Factor stayed low throughout the climb. We made most of our decisions by informal consensus. Every leadership challenge on that trip was met, although the group as a whole stayed essentially leaderless.

Keep in mind that the Pucker Factor is a situational reading and can change quickly. Let's say that our fishing buddies get lost. The Pucker Factor starts to rise a bit, and goes up more as the day begins to turn dark and cold.

As the Pucker Factor rises, the consensus process ceases to work well, especially if the group members show a wide range of competence and experience. The time needed to reach consensus is no longer available, and as the decisions to be made become more critical, it makes sense to give more authority for making them to the most competent and experienced person or persons in the group. If one of the lost fishing buddies has superior map-reading skills or has been in the area before, the group would do well to look to him for leadership, rather than debate every twist and turn in the fading light.

Now let's say the map reader finds the trail, but falls off a slippery log bridge and is dragged under a rushing torrent. The Pucker Factor escalates off the charts in seconds. One of the three remaining men needs to take hard charge and direct a rescue—*fast*.

The Pucker Factor doesn't replace your individual leadership style (you're still a sheepdog or a Volvo or a combo pizza) but lies over it. You should be able to read the situation and adjust your degree of control to fit. In most situations any of us will ever face, the Pucker Factor is neutral or close to it, and need not affect your leadership style at all. In some very safe scenarios and/or with highly competent groups, the Pucker Factor suggests informal and consensual leadership; in dire situations, it should move you to make like a Mack truck.

Leadership Style

- **Leadership is more than a set of rules and learned skills—it's an art,** one in which your individual personality plays a major role.
- **Many styles can work.** There are as many different styles of leadership as there are leaders.
- **Make use of your style.** The more aware you are of your leadership style, the better you can make use of its advantages, turn possible disadvantages into strengths, and head off any misinterpretations.
- **Your leadership style must be you.** If your style isn't authentic, group members will quickly sense the confusion and insecurity behind the faking.
- **So what's your leadership style?** Use metaphors to coax out insights.
- **Never-ever styles.** Insensitive, bullying behavior, no matter what the circumstances, is never an appropriate style. It masks a lack of self-confidence that will lead to serious mistakes in judgment.
- **Flexibility in style—the Pucker Factor.** Leadership styles need to be flexible enough to respond effectively to fast-changing situations. As the gravity of a situation increases—and/or as the competency of a group to handle that situation decreases—the leadership needs to become more authoritarian. Read the situation and adjust your degree of control to fit.

Chapter Five

Women in Leadership

Women make just as good leaders as men, but they don't lead the same way as men, and shouldn't try. The differences in the ways the two genders lead provide a rich basis for learning from each other.

In the first outdoors leadership workshop I ever gave, it was my plan to deal with the subject of women in leadership in ten minutes. I said (to an audience that was 40 percent women) that after thirty years of watching men and women lead, it seemed clear to me that both genders have the potential to become great leaders. I also said I would make no effort to customize what I taught to either men or women, because the basic principles of good leadership were the same for both—whether concerning decision making, planning, building teams, or resolving conflicts.

> Women shouldn't climb because they feel they need to prove something as women. Female or male, people should climb because they want to climb. I don't seek out other women to climb with because they are women. I climb with people I want to climb with, because of their style or personality or skills or whatever. Gender doesn't matter.
> —Sharon Wood, Adventure Dynamics,
> first North American woman to summit on Everest

Nobody challenged what I said. But the fact that I thought a few comments were enough to deal with the issue sparked a spirited discussion, led by women, that went on for two hours. Women who were just

40

gaining leadership experience, in particular, complained about lack of full acceptance of women as outdoors leaders (by men *and* women); about being disparaged by men for lack of physical strength; about feeling pressured to "act like a man" while in a leadership role; and about having to prove themselves more than did men leaders who shared the same amount of experience and level of expertise.

Older, more experienced women leaders, who had led major trips, run climbing courses, and held offices in their outdoors organizations, generally saw the same things. Many of them, however, thought that merit eventually won out. A well-trained and physically fit woman, they said, could overcome subtle and not-so-subtle prejudices, do well as a leader, and be accepted by male peers and followers.

Every workshop since has prompted the same kinds of questions, comments, and debates. This chapter is based on those discussions, plus many more conversations with other women in leadership roles.

A man's world? There's a very practical reason why the outdoors is no longer a man's world—if it ever was. Women are getting outdoors in greater numbers, buying more outdoor gear (judging from the catalogs), and tackling outdoor challenges, such as Himalayan ascents and polar expeditions, that used to be "for men only."

In the mid-1960s, the National Outdoors Leadership School (NOLS), which I founded, was the first to begin taking women on outdoors courses. There was a lot of opposition then. I remember walking into the Cowboy Bar in Jackson at that time, and having all these guys jump on me, saying, "Petzoldt, you got women doin' stuff like that?!" Sometimes the women in our courses would be carrying fifty, sixty pounds on their backs, and there were people who said that if they kept that up, they'd never be able to have children!

There's a lot of prejudice that remains about women in the outdoors. It comes from history. Too many men still want women to stay home and do the laundry. The fact is, women often do better than men in the outdoors. They've got more endurance. They're more logical, and they're more likely to make decisions that are based on reality.

—Paul Petzoldt, founder of the National Outdoor Leadership School

---

Many men are quite comfortable with this growing trend, but some are not. They resent women making inroads into the world of outdoors adventures, especially those adventures that involve superior physical strength and/or present a high degree of physical risk. It's this resentment that is the catalyst for much of the petty biases and double standards that women deplore.

If this resentment were rational, it would have ceased long ago. The argument that women lack the physical strength for outdoor adventures is particularly weak. As most of us know from our own experiences in the outdoors, the large-muscle strength of men is often a less useful physical attribute than flexibility, balance, and endurance, especially under punishing conditions. And, in any case, the physical performance gap between the genders continues to narrow, as international track and field statistics show.

■

My passion is the outdoors. I've worked in the backcountry since 1980, and now I'm lucky enough to have a job protecting the environment. I was fortunate to start my professional outdoor career on an all-women trail crew in Wyoming. Yes, there were jokes about us, but the three of us together could do anything an all-male crew could do. It was hard for me, four years later, to work with a man who wanted to push, pull, lift, chop, and saw by himself. I had learned that I was strong and that working with others made me even stronger.

Later, teaching for the National Outdoor Leadership School (NOLS), I again got to work with strong women who were great leadership role models for me. I've become very comfortable with my leadership style. However, I'll never forget the student who confided to me after a very successful course that she had been shocked to find herself thinking, after just meeting her instructor team, that the course wasn't going to be very good or very hard because two of the three instructors were women. This student considered herself a feminist and had startled herself with this impression. If she thought this, how many others have thought the same thing and never admitted it? The idea that the outdoors is a place for hard men dies hard.

—Caroline Byrd, former NOLS instructor,
presently an attorney with the Wyoming Outdoor Council

■

The prejudiced notion that taking outdoors physical risks is a "guy" thing is harder to deal with because it has been imbedded in our culture ever since the guys went out to kill saber-toothed tigers. Never mind that the biological justification for keeping women safer than men disappeared a long time ago, and that 90 percent of outdoors adventures today are less risky than crossing a busy downtown street.

The culprit is testosterone. There's no doubt that men are more driven by their hormones to search out external physical challenges than are women (look at the huge differential between car insurance rates for your teenage son and daughter). But does this make males better at tackling such risks, or give them a greater right to do so?

It's true that some first ascents probably could not have been made without the kind of suicidal zeal that drives some men. Fifty years ago, for example, male climbers threw themselves against the famous north wall routes in the Alps, but many were killed before the climbs were finally established. Does this make extreme climbing a male preserve? In my book, any adventurer who is emotionally driven past the point of being able to balance outdoors risks with the other priorities of life is either very young or a dangerous eccentric. That women rarely reach this point is to their credit.

The bottom line is that women have every right to demand an equal place in any outdoors activities, including those that involve large amounts of physical strength and/or risk. Men who still resent this right need to bring their heads and hearts, as well as their hormones, to the game. Outdoors organizations, as discussed later in this chapter, can do a lot to advance this process.

Women lead differently than men. A big mistake many men—and some women—make is to think that women must use male models to lead. While the same basic principles of leadership work for women as well as men, there are significant differences in the way the two genders apply them. Each gender tends to excel in areas in which the other doesn't.

■

I recently read a book about growing up female in America. What I remember most is the author's comment that women spend their twenties and thirties recovering from adolescence.

If I had read this when I was in the thick of my twenties and thirties, I'm not sure I would have understood. But I've been out of those decades for several years, so I know exactly what she means we were struggling to overcome: instinctive self-doubt fueled by an adolescent craving for approval, mostly from b-o-y-s.

This handicap did not help me excel as a leader. And for many of my early years in business, I sought external guidance everywhere—mostly from men—on how to be a leader. How tiring—and how futile.

Then it somehow dawned on me—sometime in my early forties—that the most important thing I could do as a leader was to trust myself—and be gently guided by my own experiences and my own clear idea of what I cared about and what I stood for.

What a relief.

—Ellen Wessel, President, Moving Comfort; Vice President, Outdoor Recreation Coalition of America

■

Tends is the operative word, because general observations often lead to stereotypes, and any stereotype is misleading. While gender differences in leadership often are significant, they can be overshadowed by differences in personality and style that have nothing to do with gender.

Still, the gender differences in leadership are so often there, they need to be acknowledged and explored. How many of these differences are with us at birth and how many are learned as we grow up are questions for the academics.

What is relevant here is to see these differences not as polar opposites but as points of emphasis along continuous lines, representing features of personality. For example, the chart below lists five personality features common to both men and women leaders. I've anchored each feature with a negative extreme at either end.

PRESENCE IN THE WORLD
egotistical _____ | _____ self-effacing

FOCUS
tunnel vision _____ | _____ distractable

FLEXIBILITY
rigid _____ | _____ waffling

DEALING WITH CONFLICT
belligerent _____ | _____ peace at any price

INCLUSIVENESS
isolated _____ | _____ overly solicitous

Good leadership for either gender means not moving too far from the center point of any of these lines. Certainly, neither gender should get stuck on the extremes. For men, more often that means the extremes on the left side of the chart: disparaging others with less experience; blinding themselves to new opportunities by overfocusing on one goal, sticking to decisions that have been overtaken by events; shouting and bullying to get their way; making no attempts to relate to team members.

When women fail, they are more likely to fall off the chart to the right: being reluctant to take charge when strong direction is called for; heading off on too many tangents at once; backtracking too easily on decisions; avoiding conflicts that should be handled; turning off team members with too much talk and attention.

In my experience, the best male leadership tends to fall somewhat to the left of center on these lines, and the best female leadership, somewhat to the right. The following example will illustrate my point.

Ann Medlock and I had been married only six months when she and I, plus our kids, were on a camping trip that I thought would be a great way for members of the new extended family to get to know one another. The trouble was, it rained. And rained. And rained. All my careful plans for a jolly trip with great views and wonderful campsites were being washed down muddy trails—or dripping down the backs of our necks.

My frustration piled up like the dark clouds that pushed in on us from all sides. All that I could see was that the weather was turning our trip into a disaster. Of course, my frustration only made matters worse, especially as I tried to hurry everyone along slippery trails the first day so we'd be sure to get to a favorite campsite before dark.

Quizzically, Ann watched my leadership efforts for a while, rain streaming off her poncho. Then she reminded me that the purpose of the trip was to have fun—so what could we do to have fun in the rain? She had plenty of ideas and started to put them into action. She got us to make up songs and tell stories. We slowed down so nobody was nervous about wet footing; we wouldn't get to the campsite I favored, but there were plenty of good places short of there. Given the lighter environment that Ann's leadership produced, my daughter's boyfriend turned out to be a Robin Williams clone, who, with a little encouragement, transformed our soggy march into "Saturday Night Live." Ann's son was so good at mimicking marmots that he was soon "talking" to a whole valleyful of the critters. Fifteen years and many family backpacks later, we probably talk more about that trip than any other.

Ann's leadership instincts in that situation were right on target; from my experience with women, I would say a good deal of what she did was gender-based. Ann was much more flexible than I, tossing out plans that had been overtaken by events. Focusing on the broader goal of having fun and bringing people together, she was also more able to see new options. And she was less likely than I to put a lot of ego into resisting the unstoppable—rain is rain, especially in the Northwest.

Another good example of women in leadership is the fight for the soul of the radical environmental group Earth First!

In the 1980s, the (male) leadership of Earth First! promoted strategies of sabotage in an effort to save the wilderness: pouring sand into gas tanks of bulldozers, breaking drilling equipment, spiking trees. Their tactics, anchored on the left extremes of the personality lines drawn in the chart above, created an uproar in the California timber industry, prompted legal crackdowns, isolated the organization from any support from the rest of the environmental movement, and resulted in the permanent protection of very few trees.

Judi Bari, a veteran labor organizer who had joined Earth First! in the late 1980s, took on the challenge of reorienting the organization away from the isolationist, macho mentality that had governed it from the beginning. She saw that the strength and future of environmental politics depended on making the group as inclusive as possible, working with loggers and not against them, and keeping tactics nonviolent. Environmentalists and loggers should be allies, not enemies; the real bad guys were the multinational corporations overcutting the forests.

Operating from that wider vision, she began organizing dialogues with loggers, opening up Earth First! to a wider membership, especially women, and channeling the group's energies into large-scale nonviolent protests, including Redwood Summer, an event that gained national attention in 1990. Her leadership, like Ann Medlock's, was right of center on the personality lines above, but not so far to the right that it lost power and relevance for the people she led.

Ironically, just as Redwood Summer and similar tactics, including California ballot initiatives, began to gain ground, Bari was almost killed when a bomb blew up her car.

Each gender can learn from the other. Both men and women need to see the differences in their leadership styles as strengths rather than weaknesses in the other—and a rich basis for learning from each other.

Pay attention to how the other gender leads. Go out of your way to watch leaders in action, and make mental note of how they tackle a certain challenge or take up a particular opportunity. If you're male, are you able to learn from women leaders how to better see connections and threads in complex and chaotic situations, deal more patiently with conflict, control your ego, and establish better personal relationships with those you lead? And if you're female, are you able to learn from men leaders how to improve your skills in detailed planning, turn ideas into policy options, and speak up in public?

The ideal leader combines traits that are generally regarded as the predominant strengths of either one or the other gender. As you learn from watching the other gender lead, you'll feel your own leadership being pulled toward an ideal center. The most effective leaders I know, or know about, draw the best from both arenas. They are logical as well as intuitive. They are able to see and make connections with other subjects and views that may not at first seem related—and they are capable of intense focus, organization, and attention to detail. They can show their feelings and sense the feelings of others—and control their emotions when necessary. They know when to lighten up, and when to press for the bottom line. They make personal and genuinely caring connections with the people they talk to and are capable of making big decisions involving fortunes and lives.

Good leaders use every aspect of their beings to lead. Some of these aspects are already strong; some need to be strengthened by training, practice, and by learning from others—including leaders of the other gender.

Women leading outdoors—and in. It's no secret that women face more cultural and societal obstacles than men in taking on leadership roles in any field. The training, experience, and self-confidence women gain as leaders in the outdoors can help them change constraining relationships at home and break through glass ceilings at work. And the appreciation men gain from following and learning from women leaders in the outdoors shapes attitudes that can improve how they deal with wives, daughters, coworkers, friends, and all the other women in their lives. This is another good example of how outdoors leadership training and experience influence a far wider world than the one up in the hills.

What outdoors organizations can do. In most outdoors organizations, the pool of women leaders is too small, too few women apply for leadership positions, and younger women have too few older women leaders as role models.

There are ways clubs can improve these numbers. For starters, they can actively recruit women for leadership roles and training classes. What is needed are not five-minute pep talks at annual meetings, but directed, long-term programs in which established women leaders spend time with prospective women leaders in small groups and one-on-one, answering their questions and urging them to take up leadership training and roles. As part of this recruitment process, outdoors organizations can create and advertise special forums for women, led by experienced women leaders, in which women can feel comfortable to ask the kinds of questions that many of them are hesitant to ask in mixed groups.

Women leaders need their own models. Organizations can amplify the role-model potential of women already leading by inviting them to write columns in club newsletters, for example, or featuring them in club presentations—and not only when the subject is gender-based.

Club policies need to explicitly welcome women in leadership roles. Organizations need to make their positions clear that they expect women to make excellent leaders on their own terms, without having to model their leadership after "the way men do it."

The guys need some help, too. Clubs can provide venues for men to talk about how they feel about women in leadership. What's a practical concern and what's prejudice? Men need to air all their views, as a way of gaining the comfort some of them lack around the issue of women leading.

Finally, outdoors organizations need to host discussions about women in leadership that involve both genders. Give people a chance to voice all their complaints and feelings—but use a facilitator to help the group explore constructive solutions as well.

HANDLING SEXIST BEHAVIOR AND SEXUAL HARASSMENT

Sexist behavior and sexual harassment on outdoors trips and in outdoors organizations do happen. Leaders should not wait until a situation arises before they think about and discuss how they and the group ought to react. The following guide incorporates many contributions from women who have faced these problems.

I use the terms *sexist behavior* and *sexual harassment* the way they are commonly used, for example, in business and in the armed forces. Sexist behavior might not be sexual at all, but rather consist of language and gestures that reflect prejudiced notions that women are incompetent or inferior. Sexual harassment means not only unwanted physical advances and touching, but offensive, sexually suggestive language as well.

Sexist behavior, of course, is not the only form of discrimination encountered by outdoor leaders. While the suggestions that follow are keyed to sexist behavior, many of them are also relevant to other forms of prejudice, including racism and ageism—the presumption of incompetency that young leaders sometimes encounter from older people on their trips.

Be alert for, and ready to react to, signs of trouble. If you're a woman leader, you know you have a problem right at the trailhead if you overhear a male member of your team joking to a friend that you might be too small to lift your pack or that you have a voice that won't carry across the trail.

Tailor the response to the offense. If the sexist behavior seems minor and incidental, you might choose to ignore it initially. There *are* gray areas in which behavior can be interpreted differently yet fairly, depending on the personalities and the circumstances.

In no case, however, should you adjust your own behavior—for example, by trying to throw your weight around and make more noise—to gain the respect of sexist males.

If you sense that the behavior is *not* minor and incidental, especially if it continues, then you must not ignore it. Nor, of course, should you ignore direct challenges to your leadership. ("We're never going to get there if we follow *her*.")

Letting this kind of behavior go unchallenged will affect more than your dignity; it can affect the morale of the group, and/or undermine group confidence in your leadership. Under these circumstances, you have no choice but to confront the offender—and the sooner the better.

Confront the offender. On the trail, the best way for you as leader to confront offensive behavior is with a calm, direct admonition to stop. ("Look, you may think your remarks about me are funny, but I don't. They're insulting, and I want you to stop.")

But that's not enough. Make sure the offender understands that his behavior is not only insulting but also irresponsible and dangerous because it undermines your authority. Your position is similar to that of an airline pilot with a passenger aboard who is loudly doubting the pilot's ability to land the plane. If a crisis develops on the trip, you're in charge, not him, and the group's confidence in your leadership becomes a key safety factor.

Tell the offender that if he has specific suggestions for the trip, he's welcome to make them just like anybody else. If not, he needs to keep his mouth shut. And if you're confronting him near the trailhead, add that unless he can shape up and support your leadership, he should head back to his car.

It's probably best initially to confront the offender out of hearing of the rest of the group. But if you see that others have noticed the out-of-line behavior and are wondering how you'll react, then you may have no choice but to confront him publicly. The point is not to go out of your way to embarrass the offender, but to reaffirm your leadership role with the group.

The offender is unlikely to expect such a cool, direct response—after all, he has probably been getting away with this behavior for years. The shock value of such a response often will be enough to correct the situation, at least for that trip.

If the behavior continues, you have no choice but to stop the trip while you enlist support from other members of your team. This kind of strong, directed action will strengthen rather than diminish your role as leader in the eyes of your group. The pressures that the group can then bring to bear on the offender should end the problem. If the offender is a member of an outdoors organization, tell him you plan to file a formal complaint.

As leader, you have no option but to confront sexual harassment, immediately and unequivocally, using the techniques described above. Then report it to your organization as soon as possible.

Too many outdoors organizations are reluctant to take strong action to investigate complaints of sexual harassment and to deal with offenders. Sometimes this reluctance comes from the biases of an old boys' network and sometimes it's simply that organizations don't want to deal with the trouble and embarrassment. But it's hard to imagine a greater disservice than an organization shoving sexual harassment under the rug, allowing the same offenders to repeat their behavior.

Sometimes women who've been harassed are reluctant to report the offense; like the organization, they may want to avoid the trouble and embarrassment. But sometimes women—especially those in extremely physical activities that are still male-dominated—keep quiet because they're afraid a formal complaint might somehow jeopardize their popularity as "one of the gang."

If that's the case, it's the gang that needs to shape up its attitudes, not just the offender. Filing and following up on a sexual harassment complaint in these circumstances takes courage. But the organization must be forced to deal with behavior and attitudes that degrade its members and undermine its own integrity.

Women in Leadership

❑ **A man's world?** Women make just as good leaders as men, and the basic principles of good leadership apply to both genders.

❑ **Women lead differently than men.** Each gender tends to excel in areas in which the other doesn't.

❑ **Each gender can learn from the other.** Both men and women need to see the differences in their leadership as strengths rather than weaknesses in the other gender—and a rich basis for learning from each other.

❑ **The ideal leader combines traits generally regarded as the predominant strengths of one gender or the other.** Good leaders use every aspect of their beings to lead.

❑ **Women leading outdoors—and in.** The training, experience, and self-confidence women gain as leaders in the outdoors can help them change constraining relationships at home and break through glass ceilings at work.

❑ **What outdoors organizations can do.** To improve the situation for women leaders, outdoors organizations can:

- *actively recruit women for leadership roles and training classes;*
- *create special forums for women and men, both together and separately, to explore constructive solutions to problems of bias;*
- *amplify the role-model potential of the women already leading;*
- *explicitly welcome women into leadership roles, making it clear that women don't have to model their leadership after "the way men do it."*

Handling Sexist Behavior and Sexual Harassment

❑ **Be alert for, and ready to react to, signs of trouble.**
❑ **Tailor the response to the offense.**
  ▪ *If the sexist behavior seems minor and incidental, you might choose to ignore it.*
  ▪ *In no case, however, should you adjust your own behavior to gain the respect of sexist males.*
  ▪ *If you sense that the offensive behavior is not minor and incidental, especially if it continues, then you must not ignore it. Nor, of course, should you ignore direct challenges to your leadership.*
❑ **Confront the offender.** On the trail, the best way to confront offensive behavior is with a calm, direct admonition to stop.
  ▪ *Make sure the offender understands that his behavior is not only insulting, but also irresponsible and dangerous because it undermines your authority.*
  ▪ *Confront the offender in public, if necessary to reaffirm your leadership role or to generate peer pressure against him.*
  ▪ *If the behavior continues, you have no choice but to stop the trip while you enlist support from other members of your team.*
❑ **Confront sexual harassment, immediately and unequivocally,** using the techniques described above. Then file, and follow up on, a formal complaint to your organization.

Chapter Six

Making Good Decisions

Systematic thinking, common sense, and intuition are the keys to making good decisions. The best decision makers use all three. But there's no such thing as a perfect decision: use both your successes and your failures to improve your choices next time around.

It can be so easy to make rash decisions, especially when you're buffeted by time pressures, competing priorities, strong emotions—or perhaps even the thought of a good meal.

———————

The 1963 Harvard ascent of Mount McKinley's north wall went straight up the center of what cartographer Bradford Washburn once called "the greatest precipice known to man." We had taken over a month to inch up the face, dodging avalanches and waiting out a major storm. We'd come down the mountain on the "easy" side in two days, then circled around to our original base camp on the Peters Glacier. From there, it was a straight shot across the tundra to our van.

It had taken us three days to pack in to base camp the month before. This time, our heads filled with thoughts of steaks and hot showers, we recrossed the mosquito-infested wilderness in two. When we reached the McKinley River in late afternoon, we could see our VW Microbus on the far side, less than a half mile away.

The water level in glacier-fed rivers such as the McKinley varies a good deal, depending on the time of day. In this case, sunlight hit the north side of the mountain in the early afternoon, melting the snow and ice and intensifying the flow into the meltwater braids and channels that became roaring creeks feeding the river. It took these surges about two hours to get to the place we'd reached on the riverbank in two days, so that when we at last got there, the river was in full flood.

There's a cardinal rule in crossing dangerous rivers like the McKinley—wait until low water. For us, that would have meant seven or eight hours. The snow and ice on the mountain would start to refreeze once the sun had disappeared, and the flows of meltwater would decrease by half. The point of the river where we needed to cross would be at its lowest in early morning. The smart move would have been to catch some sleep on the riverbank, then cross at first light.

But that was all the rational stuff. We were remembering that the manager of the McKinley Park Hotel, a man of little charm, had made a public bet that the Harvard team would never climb the north wall and live to tell about it. If our "sheer folly" succeeded, he promised to treat us to all the steak dinners we could eat. His hotel was less than an hour away, once we got to the van. We could smell those steaks.

We looked at the river rushing past us. The floodwaters were almost waist high and moving fast. The roar was so loud we had to scream into each other's ears to be heard. What to do?

We were all in our early twenties. We'd just made the first direct ascent of one of the highest and most dangerous mountain walls in the world. We were indestructible. We were unstoppable. And we wanted our steaks. Waiting for low water would have been prudent, but it also would have required patience we didn't have. We decided to cross.

We cut balance poles from trees along the riverbank, roped up in one team of three and two teams of two, and started across the eleven braided streams that formed the river. The poles, plus the weight of our packs, helped us keep our footing as we crossed the first ten streams without incident.

Hank Abrons and I were the last team to reach the final braid. Hank plunged in and was almost across when I started in. Almost at once I stepped into a hole that the others had somehow missed, lost my balance, and was dragged under. I struggled to get my face above water, gasping for air, but my pack had now become a deadly anchor. Tons of fast-moving water pummeled me against rocks on the stream bottom. Swimming was impossible. Hank, now on the far bank, was pulled off his feet by the rope that joined us, and dragged backward across the gravel bar toward the flood. The others were too far away to help in time. In the next thirty seconds, either the pull of the rope would pendulum me onto the far bank, or I would pull Hank into the river, too—and we both would drown.

Hank spread-eagled himself on the bank, desperately trying to anchor his body, but there were no pieces of driftwood or large rocks on this stretch of the river, and he was pulled foot by foot closer to the edge. I was helpless, one moment smashed against the rocks on the river bottom, then up, clawing for air.

I hit the far bank just as Hank was being dragged the final few feet into the river. Lying on the cold gravel, battered and gasping, I felt the sting of a hundred minor cuts and bruises. No bones were broken, however, and after a cup of hot tea and a change into dry clothes, the warmth slowly returned to my body.

We drove eighteen miles to the McKinley Park Hotel, heading for the steaks that Hank and I had almost died for. After the seven of us finished off two dinners apiece, the manager, a poor loser, expressed his disappointment that the mountain hadn't finished us off.

■

To train people to make good decisions in the outdoors, you've got to take them into the outdoors, into real situations, and let them face challenges by themselves. They learn soon enough that if they make foolish decisions, or if they base their decisions on "hope" or "faith" that things will work out—they fail. And if they make decisions based on reality, they succeed.
—Paul Petzoldt, founder of the National Outdoor Leadership School

■

Every once in a while I'll think of those desperate seconds in that roaring flood. It's easy, in retrospect, to dismiss that decision to cross the river at high water as the foolish actions of youth, but that begs the question. What if, sitting on that far bank, thinking of those steaks, we'd had enough training in decision-making skills to temper our rashness, focus on the odds, and more accurately consider what we were about to do? Sure, we still might have gone ahead, so strong was our bravado. But maybe not.

Ours was a common mistake. Many, perhaps most, of the people who put themselves in potentially dangerous situations in the outdoors are no wiser or better trained than we were. And, to be fair, gray hair is no guarantee against making stupid decisions—wherever you are.

In the years since that Alaskan experience, I've made many big decisions—in the outdoors, in Vietnam, at the United Nations, and in my personal life. Some of these decisions were bad and some were good, but I've learned from all of them along the way. Here is the advice I wish I'd had as a young man, sitting on a rock on the bank of the McKinley River, wondering whether or not to risk my life for a steak:

Anticipate decisions before you have to make them. Anticipating decisions allows you to plan ahead, to get a jump on creating and sometimes even testing options. Sometimes the need for a tough decision can be removed completely.

If, back at base camp, we had anticipated the importance of the river's height on that McKinley trip, we might have paced ourselves to arrive at the crossing at low water. (Whether we would have had the discipline to actually do that is another matter!)

If your weather radio, or your weather sense, says a storm front is moving in, then start thinking early about the decision you'll have to make that night about where to camp. On which side of the ridge are you most likely to find tree cover? Where will it be easiest to rig tarps to keep your cook space dry?

Effectively manage the time you have in which to make your decision. It's not as simple as merely making sure time doesn't run out; making a decision too soon can sometimes cause as many problems as making one too late, especially in very fluid situations where factors such as weather are changing rapidly.

In timing a decision, the best course of action is to:
- consider your overall schedule. What's your fail-safe point—the latest possible hour at which you must end your activity (for example, be back at your car, reach a rendezvous, or avoid being caught out after dark)?
- determine the time it will take to implement each of the options you're considering; then
- subtract the time needed to implement the *slowest* option from the fail-safe hour to determine the latest point before which your decision must be made.

Let's say, for example, that you're leading a scramble up a peak of middling difficulty. By the end of the first day, you get your group to the standard camping place, high on the ridge, for a summit try the next morning. When you awake at 6:00 A.M., however, there's a total whiteout—you can hardly see your hand in front of your face. If conditions hold, there will be no point in trying to complete the climb. You'll face serious routefinding problems—especially on the way down from the summit—and, of course, there will be no views.

By the time all the members of your team have eaten breakfast, taken down their tents, and put on their climbing gear, it's 7:00 A.M. You know you have to be back at your cars by 6:00 P.M. at the latest, and that in the whiteout your camp is four hours from the road. You also know that, should the weather break, the trip up to the summit and back down to the cars will take nine hours. Applying the decision-making strategy given above, you subtract nine hours from 6:00 P.M. and reason that you have until 9:00

A.M.—two more hours before you have to decide whether or not to abandon the summit try. Since whiteouts can suddenly lift, it makes sense to wait until the absolutely last possible moment. The rest of your decision will be easy: simply go or don't go depending on the weather at 9:00 A.M.

Try this decision-making strategy. Most outdoor decisions, however, can't be anticipated away, or reduced to the single element of timing. For years I've watched experienced outdoors people, including myself, make complex decisions. From all this observation and experience I've developed a strategy that will work for anyone.

- Start by stopping—take a breath; center yourself
- Make a preliminary scan of options
- Look for unconventional options; develop 360-degree vision
- Get the best information you can about each option
- Use this information to define the risks and benefits of each option
- Assign a relative weight to each risk and benefit, in order to compare them to one another
- Pick the option whose benefits most outweigh its risks
- Implement the decision
- Adjust your decision to reflect new information

Search and rescue operations occasionally require making life and death decisions. For example, in avalanche rescue, if the buried people weren't wearing transceivers and you don't have a rescue dog, then you have to physically probe for buried bodies using a line of searchers wielding long sticks called avalanche probes. One of the trade-offs in using probes is that if you probe deeply, more than 2 meters, it can take a lot more time than if you do a shallow probe.

And statistically, we know that a person buried at the bottom of an avalanche is often crushed physically, and much less likely to be alive than one buried near the surface. So you could be wasting valuable minutes by ordering a deep probe.

It's a matter of playing the odds. By ordering your team *not* to probe beyond 2 meters, you may be signing the death warrant of any person buried deeper than that.

In land search, it's the same. You focus your resources on the most likely areas. It's the right thing to do, but you could miss somebody if he or she is in a less likely area.

A leader has to have the guts to make decisions like these. You make them, and then just get on with it. You can't second-guess.

—Tim Auger, Public Safety Specialist,
Search and Rescue, Banff National Park

I know you're not going to be making decisions in the outdoors with a pencil and paper, balancing a pocket calculator on your knee in the middle of a blizzard. With experience, however, this decision-making strategy becomes seamless and reflexive—defining options, weighting costs and benefits, then making the choice.

I've slowed down the process here so you can see more clearly how it works. In the real world, however, it moves as fast as it needs to move. If time is short, as it often is in outdoor leadership situations, you may have to collapse all these steps into minutes—or even seconds. You do the best you can in the time available.

To make this strategy work for you, you may need to discipline your mind a little more than most of us are used to. The results justify the effort. And as the process becomes second nature, it moves faster and easier. Here—in slow motion—is how it works.

Start by stopping. Do whatever you need to do to calm yourself. Count to ten. Take a deep breath. Whatever happens next depends on how centered and aware you are.

Make a preliminary scan of options. Let's say you're leading a hike in rough country and the trail leads to a log bridge over a swiftly flowing stream. The log looks slippery. There are no alternative crossings in sight. What should you do? Right away, you can see two options:

- risk crossing on the log, or
- look for an easier crossing.

Look for unconventional options. Are there any other options you've missed? Your thinking process has been fairly conventional so far. How can you widen your search?

Most of us tend to develop standard thought patterns for addressing decisions in our lives. We tend to go down the same mental checklists, rely on the advice of the same friends, look to standard written sources, and sort through our own previous experiences. This is all reasonable, because our standard patterns probably work well for us 90 percent of the time, and it makes sense to rely on them. The problem is the other 10 percent. Looking at that slippery log, you need to move beyond the search patterns you already know and trust. Learn to develop 360-degree vision for any environment in which you find yourself.

Think old "Star Trek" reruns. The starship *Enterprise* is in some convoluted crisis involving alternative realities. The crew tries to plug in conventional options (like firing a photon torpedo at the bad guys), but these either don't work or make matters worse. Finally one of the crew breaks the rules and does something completely off-the-wall—and it succeeds.

A good rule of thumb, whether you have five seconds or five hours in which to make a decision, is to spend only about half the time sifting through conventional options—those that are obvious or that you've used before or seen others use. Then, no matter how successful you think your search has been, consciously transfer your focus from the conventional to the unconventional. What's a way to solve this problem that is so different or counterintuitive that it keeps getting overlooked or ruled out when you do things by the book?

I was on a whale-watching trip in Alaska a few years ago, and at one point three of us were out in a Zodiak, a light rubber boat powered by an outboard motor. When one of the whales surfaced right in front of us, my friend in the stern cut the throttle too fast and the little boat took on so much water, it started to swamp. We had perhaps ten seconds to start bailing—or swimming. We took a few of those seconds to survey the vessel, looking for a bailing can; there was none. Spending more time searching for the nonexistent can would have been fruitless. What else would hold water? Hands were too small. Hats were too porous. But we all were wearing rubber boots. We took off one boot apiece and bailed like crazy. The boat was soon dry, at the price of only three cold feet!

Back to that slippery log. In this case, your problem is not that you initially seem to have no options (as in the Zodiak example). You have at least two. But are they the best ones? Is there one you've missed?

It's a bright, sunny day. The stream's fast but might well be wadeable. There's a gravel bar on the other side. You have a climbing rope. You could send one of your stronger members over with one end of the rope to make a handrail by stretching it taut between trees on opposite banks. Then everybody could take off their boots, roll up their pants, wade across, and dry off on the far bank while you eat lunch. Well—why not?

Get the best possible information about each option. Now you have three options. The next step is to develop as much information as possible about each one in the time available. For this, you need to ask key questions, each targeted at a significant unknown. Here is where that 360-degree view comes in handy again.

- How likely is a fall off the log?
- How bad are the consequences of such a fall?
- Are there good alternative crossings?
- How difficult is the ford if you wade?
- Will any team members panic, crossing the log or fording the stream, even if it's safe?
- Are you under time pressure?

Now you need to answer these questions. In fifteen minutes you're able to find out that:

- a fall is a real possibility—that log is really slippery;
- the consequences of a fall would be a good dunking in cold water and some bruises; there's some risk of a twisted ankle, but drowning is not a possibility;
- there is what appears to be a wider log 100 yards upstream, but the path to it lies through heavy brush and nettles;
- wading across would be exciting, but doable; the worst that could happen would be a good dunking in cold water;
- one of the beginners might panic with either the log or the ford, but it would be easier to fish him out from the ford;
- there's no time pressure—you're well ahead of schedule.

Use this information to define the risks and benefits of each option. If you wrote this down on paper, it would look something like this:

OPTION 1: Cross on the Log

Risks	Benefits
Someone might fall off and get hurt	Gets you across the stream
Someone might panic	

OPTION 2: Take Alternative Crossing

Risks	Benefits
Nasty bushwhack	Gets you across the stream
Someone might fall off and get hurt	
Creates a thirty-minute delay	

OPTION 3: Wade Across

Risks	Benefits
Someone might fall into the stream	Gets you across the stream
Someone might panic	Creates a relatively safe,
Creates a forty-five-minute delay	adventurous, and pleasurable experience

Assign a relative weight to each risk and benefit, in order to compare them. Comparing risks and benefits may seem like comparing apples and oranges. How do you rate the negative effect of a nasty bushwhack against the benefit of a safer trip across a log? How much of a delay justifies an increased chance of a fall?

The only way to deal with comparison problems such as these is to do what stockbrokers, insurance analysts, and professional gamblers do every day: assign a relative weight to each risk and benefit. Weight is the product of two factors:

1) the *probability* that that risk or benefit will happen or is true. (How likely is it that someone will fall off that first log? How likely is it that the second log is safer?) For outdoors decisions, it's usually enough to rate probabilities roughly, say, from 1 (low) to 3 (high).

2) the *relative importance* you place on each risk and benefit. (How serious would a fall down in a ford be? How important is it that we cross as fast as possible?) Rate relative importances also from 1 (low) to 3 (high).

Weight = probability x relative importance. Risks or benefits that are very likely to happen (3) and of high importance (3) get a high weight (9). Those unlikely to happen (1) and of little importance if they did (1), get a low weight (1). You can fine-tune the analyses as much as you like, using broader scales (1 to 5, for example).

Estimate probabilities by using the research you've already done. Estimate the relative importance of each risk or benefit by talking to members of your group, if there's time, or by using your own sense of the group if there isn't. When you apply this to your log crossing example, the whole set-up looks like this (P = probability; RI = relative importance; Wt = weight):

OPTION 1: Cross on the Log

Risks	P RI Wt	Benefits	P RI Wt
Someone might fall off and get hurt	3 x 3 = 9	Gets you across the stream	3 x 3 = 9
Someone might panic	1 x 2 = 2		
Total	11	Total	9

OPTION 2: Take Alternative Log

Risks	P RI Wt	Benefits	P RI Wt
Nasty bushwhack	3 x 2 = 6	Gets you across the stream	3 x 3 = 9
Someone might fall off and get hurt	1 x 3 = 3		
Creates a 30-minute delay	3 x 1 = 3		
Total	12	Total	9

OPTION 3: Wade Across

Risks	P RI Wt	Benefits	P RI Wt
Someone might fall down in the stream	1 x 2 = 2	Gets you across the stream	3 x 3 = 9
Someone might panic	1 x 2 = 2	Relatively safe, adventurous, and pleasant experience	2 x 2 = 4
Creates a 45-minute delay	3 x 1 = 3		
Total	7	Total	13

Pick the option whose benefits most outweigh its risks. In this case, Option 3 seems to be the best bet, as it carries a benefit the other two lack. And while it has more risks than the other two, none of them seem serious.

But notice the swing factors. The relative importances you've assigned are key in making your decision—and are completely dependent on value judgments that might vary from group to group. Your decision might be quite different, for example, if you were with a group who made it clear that they wanted to avoid getting wet at all costs but didn't mind bush-whacking. For them, Option 2 might be the best choice. And if you were under severe time pressure, Option 1 might be best.

Again, I'm not suggesting for a moment that you take a clipboard and yellow pad into the bush; it's a way of *thinking* about decisions that I'm championing here. Think options. Think unconventional options. Think risks and benefits—then weight each one by assigning a probability and relative importance.

▪

In 1984, on the north side of Mount Everest, we had eight really good climbers, some of whom had been on Everest before but had failed to make the summit, and some for whom this was their first attempt. We knew that on this trip only three of them could go on to the summit. The others would have to act as a support team.

I had to make the decision of who would be on the summit team. I talked it over with people. Some felt that the younger climbers should get their shot, since the older ones had already had theirs. Others felt that those who'd been high on Everest before would have a greater chance for success. I decided in favor of experience, even though it meant turning down my own son.

It's so important to talk to people in making decisions like this. Do it one-on-one, if there's time. You have to get people's input and feelings. If you do it this way, then, when the decision's made, you've got a much better chance of rallying everyone forward as a team, with people knowing that every role, including the support roles, counts. Then you can draw everybody together, and get the best out of them.

—Lou Whittaker, climber/guide, President of Rainier Mountaineering Inc. and author of *Lou Whittaker: Memoirs of a Mountain Guide*

▪

At its most basic, what this system says is: if any risk or benefit of the options you have seems both likely and significant, then consider it seriously in making your decision. If any risk or benefit seems of low importance and probably won't happen anyway, then disregard it.

Implement the decision. The final step in the decision-making process is the same as in a golf swing: follow through. I've seen great decisions lead to poor outcomes because the right option was chosen but never effectively communicated or set in motion. Once your decision is made, create a plan for its implementation, including delegating responsibilities to other team members. Then move full speed ahead, with the confidence that you've done your best.

Adjust your decision to reflect new information. Situations can change quickly, especially in the outdoors. Be willing to make timely adjustments as your decision is being implemented. Good leaders adjust their plans to reflect new information or perspectives, but they don't cave in to pressure, and they don't act just to please others or to avoid conflict. In the stream-crossing example, you may discover that one channel in the stream is too deep to wade, a sound reason to try another option. But if the stream *is* wadeable and one person still slips and falls in, while others hesitate—that is cause for a helping hand, not for turning back.

Never let any system make the decision for you. Using systematic thinking to help you assemble and weigh options, risks, and benefits can be critical. But never go on automatic pilot. No system should ever make a decision for you. Think GIGO—garbage in equals garbage out. If the weights assigned to either risks or benefits are way off, your decision will be, too.

There are two useful checks and balances here. The first is to ask whether what you intend to do is within the realm of common sense. We've all had experiences of missing the forest for the trees, creating thought patterns that were internally consistent but based on premises that were utterly wrong.

The second check and balance is to always leave room for the nonrational doubt. Listen to your intuition. Honor your hunches. This is where decision making becomes art.

Some of what people call intuition is really tapping into our collected experiences at an unconscious level. This subtle probing of old memories is what prompts us to think the weather is about to change even though the sky is blue, or to know that the game trail we're following will never go back to the river, or to be confident that the rock we're on will yield some climbable chimneys higher up. We may not be able to completely identify the source of such knowledge, but that makes it no less persuasive.

But some of intuition doesn't seem to be tied to memory or experience at all. It's more gut instinct: something just *feels* right—or wrong. A good example is crossing a glacier full of hidden crevasses, where practically every step requires a decision to bob or weave. There are plenty of rational moves to make, such as looking for overall crack patterns in the glacier, or watching for subtle differences in shadows or melt patterns. But time and again, experienced mountaineers will turn right or left or double back with nothing to guide them but their own instinct.

You can't learn intuition from this or any other book, but this doesn't mean that intuition isn't crucial to decision making, and leadership. You can gain many insights from watching how experienced leaders balance intellect and intuition. But the best way to learn how to identify, trust, and use intuition is to develop your own track record. Keep a log of your hunches, especially on outdoors trips, whether you act on them or not. How often, in retrospect, were your hunches right on? How often were they not intuition at all, but rather the voices of fatigue or fear? By keeping a record over time, you'll build confidence in identifying and trusting your own inner voices.

Have no regrets, if you've done your best. Use both your successes and your failures to improve your decision making next time around. There's no such thing as a perfect decision. You do the best you can, with the tools available. There's no way you can accurately see all the elements that are about to determine your future.

In climbing Aconcagua we allow for five days of bad weather. One year we'd used up three of those five days, trapped in our tents at 19,000 feet. At three o'clock the next morning—our go/no-go point—I decided that the weather was still too bad for a summit try. When we woke up at seven o'clock, however, it was a perfect climbing day. We could see another party already well on their way to the summit.

All you can do in a case like this is laugh it off. You make the best decision you can with the knowledge and experience you have. Sometimes you're going to guess wrong. Sometimes you're just going to screw up. (In this case, I got a reprieve; the next day was good weather, too.)
—Peter Whittaker, climber/guide, Summits Adventure Travel

Making Good Decisions

❑ **Anticipate decisions before you have to make them.**

❑ **Effectively manage the time available in which to make your decision;** making a decision too soon can be as bad as making one too late, especially in fluid situations.

❑ **Try the following decision-making strategy.**
  - *Start by stopping*—take a breath; center yourself;
  - *Make a preliminary scan of options;*
  - *Look for unconventional options;* develop 360-degree vision;
  - *Get the best available information about each option;*
  - *Use this information to define the risks and benefits of each option;*
  - *Assign a relative weight to each risk and benefit, so they can be compared to one another.* Weight = probability x relative importance;
  - *Pick the option whose benefits most outweigh its risks,* but notice the swing factors;
  - *Implement the decision;*
  - *Adjust your decision to reflect new information.*

❑ **Never let any system make the decision for you.**
  - *Always ask whether what you intend to do is within the realm of common sense.*
  - *Listen to your intuition.* Learn to trust it by keeping a log of your hunches, whether you act on them or not. Watch how experienced leaders balance intellect and intuition.

❑ **Have no regrets, if you've done your best.** Use both your successes and your failures to improve your decision making next time around.

Chapter Seven

Caring Leadership

If you think that caring is not part of a leader's job—that it's too "soft" a quality to emphasize in the "hard" business of leading—then think again. Good leaders not only care for those they lead, they also see any trip or event as an opportunity to help people learn and grow.

Caring in the outdoors means the same as it does anyplace else: the willingness to put yourself in another's shoes, to feel compassion, to accept another's well-being as a priority of your own.

Caring leadership entails putting these qualities to work as you lead. For example:

You're leading a hike through an old-growth forest in which the terrain is gentle but the trails are poor. You're mildly concerned about arriving late at your planned campsite, with only fading light to set up camp and cook a meal. You tell the group of your concern and ask them to hurry up.

Two miles short of your destination, the trail crosses an old slide area, and for 15 feet traverses a steep dirt slope above a rushing river. Hikers before you have stamped out a path no more than a foot wide across the slope. It's a little airy, but it looks safe enough and you lead your group across. Everybody makes it easily—except Tom.

When you look back, Tom is on the far side of the traverse, afraid to cross. Shouts and gestures of encouragement from everybody only seem to embarrass him. Every instinct in you, except one, tells

66

you to join the chorus of "You can do it's!" in the hope of forcing him to snap out of his fear and make the move.

But there's one instinct that moves you in the other direction, that takes you out of your own boots and puts you into Tom's.

You hadn't met Tom before today, but from your few phone conversations you sensed he is a cautious man. Going on this backpacking trip may be the most adventuresome activity he has ever tried in his life.

Standing inside Tom's shoes, you realize how overwhelmed he is by what you're asking him to do—and how embarrassed by his fear. You also realize that if he turns back on this one, he may never go into the mountains again. So there's quite a bit at stake for him here—more than enough to justify finishing dinner by flashlight, if you have to.

You yell across to Tom to sit down and take a break. Then you get the rest of your team to focus on solving the problem instead of criticizing him. There are a few grumbles, but by and large the team agrees with you, and soon comes up with a good plan.

You and Alice, another experienced hiker, go back across the traverse. You both sit down with Tom and spend the first few minutes listening to his concerns. You tell him that his fear is completely understandable, given that this is his first time on rough terrain. Both you and Alice tell him of times you backed off moves you thought beyond your capability.

When you sense he has calmed down some, you tell him you have a plan. The more frightened Tom is, the more important it is to describe all the details; frightened people find great comfort in the specifics of answers to their fear. You tell Tom that you'll go first across the traverse, and reach back with your left hand to take his right. Then he will reach behind with his left hand and grab Alice's right. The three of you will shuffle across, so he will never have to cross his feet, which is what he told you scares him most. You'll return for his pack later.

You all practice the moves on a safe part of the trail, until Tom is ready. Then you go. You finish up your leader's responsibilities that night over coffee with a couple of quiet, private words with Tom, to make sure he's OK. When he thanks you, he is thanking you for a whole lot more than just getting him to camp.

Caring leadership is:
- *putting yourself in others' shoes, and being sensitive to their needs.*
  Use the trip sign-up calls to begin to gather a sense of who's on your team, and follow up with informal conversations on the trail.

There's no need to be intrusive, but pick up what you can about personality, style, and priorities so you can be more sensitive to people's needs, especially if trouble should ever develop. In this example, knowing that Tom is a cautious fellow informs your moves when you have to help him.

You need to be sensitive to all the elements of Tom's predicament. For you, perhaps, the traverse is almost trivial, so you must make a focused effort to sense the fear, frustration, and embarrassment that Tom is probably feeling. And because you know that panicked people often are more afraid of what they *don't* know than of what they do, you describe in detail exactly how your proposed solution will work.

- *being vulnerable.* Putting yourself into another's shoes often means sharing personal experiences of your own. Telling Tom of your own experiences of fear may feel awkward to you, but it helps put him at ease.
- *listening.* Caring communications must go both ways. Nothing demonstrates caring better than active, nonjudgmental listening. Letting Tom talk out his fear, without your comment, helps reduce his embarrassment.
- *putting caring into action.* Intentions are never enough. Tom is so afraid of a physical challenge that he becomes paralyzed. Your response is to figure out a solution, describe it in detail, practice it, and then carry it out.
- *following through.* Caring is about forming and maintaining relationships, beyond one or two wonderful gestures. Your role with Tom is not that of a bountiful majesty but of a committed and generous friend. Checking in with him that evening lets him know that you see the incident as more than simply getting someone out of a momentary jam. He appreciates that you understand the importance to him of what happened, and that you genuinely care that he is now OK.
- *letting go of judgments.* Caring includes being tolerant of the weaknesses and shortcomings of others. Tom "failed" in a way, but criticizing him clearly would have made matters worse; he probably felt bad enough.
- *caring for beginners.* Prepare for beginners' mistakes. Make sure your corrections and instructions to beginners such as Tom leave them more, not less, confident. Remember: many times these are the people who will be helping you lead next year.

In addition to the points raised in this story, caring leadership includes:
- *correcting with caring.* When you have to correct the technique or

behavior of a member of your team, try to do so in private, unless there's a general lesson that could benefit others. If Ned keeps talking loudly about his stock market strategies after you've just walked into a magnificent grove of old trees, and he fails to see that everybody else has fallen silent, approach him and put a finger to your lips, rather than shout at him to shut up from 20 feet away. On the other hand, if Molly is rigging her rappel brake the wrong way, and you see that others are having similar problems, call your team around while you show everyone how to thread the ropes correctly.

- *acknowledging others for their strengths and contributions— especially those whose strengths and contributions may be few.* Marvin may be the slowest, most poorly organized, and dullest member of your group, but what he knows about insects would fill a book. Stop for a break someplace where the bees are buzzing and ask Marvin to explain what's going on. Then thank him in front of the group; it's a small thing, but it'll make his day.
- *caring for yourself.* If you're the one who has made a mistake, don't beat yourself up over it—you're human. And give yourself credit for all the times you do it right.

■

Never criticize people in front of the group, unless you're in a life-threatening circumstance.

And never surprise people with bad news. If you're leading a trip, for example, and somebody is beginning to fall behind, don't just wait until the next break and then tell that person he or she has to go down. Talk to them as soon as you see they're in trouble. Ask them how they're feeling. Praise them for getting up that far. Offer them some suggestions on breathing or pace that will help them go further. Give them a chance to do better. Tell them, "We'll see how it goes." If things don't get better, ask them for their view on whether or not they should continue. Very often the person will then make his or her own decision to quit, and feel a lot better about it than if you ordered them to go down. Of course, if the person doesn't see it that way, you may have to lay down the law, but at least you've tried. This same approach works in business, by the way, with employees who are having a hard time meeting standards.

No matter what happens, never write people off. They may not be great climbers, or whatever, but they've got other good attributes, and you may well be working with them on something else.

—Lou Whittaker, climber/guide, President, Rainier Mountaineering Inc. and author of *Lou Whittaker: Memoirs of a Mountain Guide*

■

In mid-1996, I was climbing Mount McKinley with a team of people of mixed experience and ability, including a man from Dallas who'd never been above 10,000 feet. This guy had done quite well all the way up, but had halted just short of the summit, afraid to cross an airy traverse where a slip could mean a very long fall. He walked over to the traverse, took one look, and was too frightened to go any farther. It was as if all the fears of the entire climb suddenly descended upon him in that one moment. Frustrated and scared, he sat down in the snow and cried.

I sat down with him and started talking to him in a calm voice. I told him how close to the summit we were. I showed him that all he had to do was follow the footsteps of the rest of the team—he really was quite secure. Then I told him about some people I knew who had come very close to summits and not gone on—and regretted it for years. He listened quietly. Then he fought past his fear and went on to the top. He was absolutely thrilled.

How could I have acted otherwise? Anybody who will not take the time to help someone in that position has forgotten that we've all been scared, at some time in our lives.

As a leader, you have to be vulnerable. You can't put yourself on a pedestal. You must be accessible to the people around you, making them understand that you're human, too. The most effective leaders are the ones who can say, "I've been there." That helps others know that, like you, they can overcome the obstacles and achieve what you have achieved.

Good leaders get a tremendous amount of satisfaction from watching people grow and achieve life goals.

—Laura Evans, President/CEO, Expeditions Inspiration
and author of *The Climb of My Life*

Caring is in your interests, too. In the example with Tom, you went out of your way—some people might say way out of your way—to accommodate the needs of a single, scared beginner. Caring leadership almost always demands extra focus, sensitivity, commitment, energy, and time. So why do it?

There are two reasons. The first is that caring is a moral value. The second is that caring is a practical, powerful tool for good leadership. The first reason is your business. The second is a central theme of this book.

Caring is a practical, powerful tool for good leadership because it builds trust, provides early warning of problems, brings people together, and is a powerful tool for dealing with conflict.

Caring builds trust. Leaders must be trusted by those they lead. Especially if trouble brews and difficult decisions need to be made and carried out, trust forms a vital link between the leader and those being led—in improving communication, calming fears, strengthening cooperation, and inspiring people to perform at their best. Look to your own experience: when trust exists, people give their leader the benefit of the doubt in a crisis. When trust is absent, conflict often results.

Caring is the key to building trust. A caring attitude on your part promotes trust in your leadership more than any other factor, including technical competence. If people know you care, that their needs and interests matter to you, they become more comfortable following your lead, readier to produce their best effort, and more likely to give you the benefit of the doubt when difficult decisions must be made.

The trust-building impact of caring spreads in your team like leaven in bread. In the example we started with, it isn't only Tom whose trust in you is dramatically increased by the fifteen minutes you spent getting him across the traverse and helping him save face. Everybody in your group saw what you did and trusts you more because of the caring you showed— even those who initially may have opposed what you wanted to do. They now know that if the group gets into any kind of jam, or if anyone has an accident or makes a mistake, you'll deal with the situation with the same degree of caring that you showed Tom. That increases the comfort they feel around you and the trust they have in you as leader.

The incident will also increase their trust in your judgment. When they saw you deliberately delay an already late trip to find a solution for Tom that was not only effective but compassionate, they saw you weighing options in a very wise way. And they were impressed by the lesson. They saw you looking 360 degrees, weighing soft as well as hard factors. They saw how you focused on the group's well-being while simultaneously constructing a sensitive and sensible solution to a serious problem for one member. There's a pleasing completeness to people who lead this way that inspires trust in anyone who shows it.

Finally, your group members now also trust you more as leader because they saw you actually *lead*. While you may have been tempted, you didn't join the chorus of unhelpful shouts but instead helped the group focus their minds and energies on doing what was the right thing to do. They saw you make a difficult decision and carry it out.

This close linkage between caring and trust also works in reverse.

I was on a climb once when our group ran into Al, a mountaineer I knew, heading down the route we had just come up. Al said he was leading a scrambling group that, in his opinion, was the slowest, most namby-pamby, complaining bunch of people he'd ever had the misfortune to take into the mountains. They were so horrible, he continued, that he'd left them a mile back on the trail. The direction down to the cars was clear; it followed an obvious stream. There was plenty of time. They could damn well get down on their own. He'd had it.

The trail down was poor and, at that time of year, overgrown with nettles and slide alder. Al knew the track well; the rest of his group didn't. By leaving them behind, he was dooming them to a terrible three-hour bushwhack. A richly deserved punishment for their incompetence, he said, as he headed down.

––––––––––––––––

The only one who got "punished," of course, was Al. The least of it was getting hauled on the carpet by his club for his breach of safety standards. The real punishment was that the incident completely undermined whatever trust people had had in him as a leader. Nobody wanted to go out with Al from that trip on, despite his vast experience and considerable technical skill. People feared, quite rightly, that if they didn't measure up to Al's standards, he'd abandon them to fight the nettles—or worse.

Caring provides an early warning system. Caring helps you be more sensitive early on to behaviors and conditions that might affect the success of your trip.

––––––––––––––––

Sarah is a new member of your club and the first trip she signs up for is yours. At the trailhead, you notice that she's quite proud of a brand new pair of boots. Fine boots or not, you know that new footwear sometimes means trouble, so you check in with her several times during the first mile or two, asking her how she's doing. She tells you she's fine—in a tone of voice that suggests you mind your own business.

Most leaders would leave it at that. But your assessment of Sarah is that she's a person of tight-lipped stubbornness, with a very proud and independent spirit. Moreover, the way she was showing off her boots earlier might make her hesitate to admit that she could ever have a problem with them. In short, you're afraid Sarah won't tell you she is having a problem.

And this is a four-day trip. Anyone with serious foot problems on the first day could be in for a truly nasty time—and could slow the group down considerably. Your fears are confirmed when you see Sarah favoring her right foot. You suspect she is developing a blister and that she won't say anything until it's too late to prevent a real problem.

At the next break, you make a show of taking off your own boots to check your feet, informally commenting that this might be a good idea for everybody. Several other people follow your lead, which leaves an opening for Sarah to do the same. You bring out the moleskin and help her treat the red spot on her heel.

Sure, Sarah should have dealt with her problem in a more mature way. Al undoubtedly would have let her limp on as payment for her foolishness. But you understood that everybody has their quirks; you were able to help Sarah get by hers, without judging her. And by caring for Sarah as a person, quirks and all, you short-circuited a potentially serious problem for the group as well as for her.

In retrospect, a little more directed caring with Tom, in the first example, might have short-circuited the problem you eventually faced there. Knowing of his cautious nature, and assuming you knew in advance about that airy traverse, you could have shown it to him on the map, then talked to him about it and listened to his concerns. Often, eliminating the element of surprise is all that needs to be done to get people like Tom over rough spots.

Caring brings people together. Look for, or create, opportunities for team members to develop caring relationships with one another. You don't need to create a social club on every outdoors trip. And if you have loners along who want to stay that way, fine. But there's considerable value in promoting caring links among team members: not only does it make the trip more fun, it has direct practical consequences as well. The more team members feel at ease with, and appreciate, each other, the better they'll perform together. That could make all the difference if you get into a crisis situation in which your ragtag bunch suddenly has to perform like a practiced team.

Start building these relationships early, with introductions at the trailhead or at the first meeting of a new group.

Everybody has their favorite way to break the ice with a group of people who don't already know each other. My favorite is to have people introduce themselves by saying their first names, followed by the name of a fruit or vegetable that starts with the same letter as their first names. One person starts, and then each subsequent person has to repeat all the previous names. For example, the fourth person might say, "Glad to meet you, Sarah Strawberry, Ted Turnip, and Ned Nectarine. My name is Charlie Chard."

Without being intrusive, look for additional opportunities as the trip progresses. These might include everything from a bit of horseplay at the stream crossing, to a half hour of sitting on a warm rock, swapping stories. Use the breaks as opportunities to help group members further introduce themselves to each other: "Charlie, did you know that Carol went to the University of Michigan, too?"

Caring can be a powerful tool for dealing with conflict. A caring approach to opponents, and to difficult people of any kind, can help defuse anger and fear enough so that both sides will be willing to risk the honest dialogue needed to achieve lasting solutions. This issue is covered in depth in Chapters Twelve and Fifteen.

Part of the power of caring in conflict situations is simply its shock value. Most people deal with conflict by using a strategy that implies, "For me to win, you have to lose." Genuinely caring words and actions sometimes surprise opponents enough to throw them off these old win/lose strategies. This can leave the door open, at least temporarily, for initiatives aimed at creating solutions that benefit all sides.

For all these reasons, caring counts. Not just soothing words, but a genuine willingness and ability to put yourself in another's shoes. Caring is an essential tool for quality leadership, bringing benefits well worth whatever extra time and attention they might cost. Caring enriches your life as much as the lives of those you care for.

■

I have three rules for leaders in the outdoors:
- You have to know where the people you're leading are coming from.
- You have to know what you want to do with them.
- And you have to love them.

You have to be unselfish. A selfish leader is a danger to both him- or herself, and to others. If I get an application from someone who wants to lead for NOLS (the National Outdoor Leadership School) and I know that that person is selfish, I throw the application away. You can't have leaders who will make plans based just on their personal preferences rather than on what's needed and wanted for the program or group.

You can teach people to be unselfish. You start by getting them to see all the damage they're doing to themselves by being selfish. If you're selfish, you'll never have any real companions, and you'll never get people to help you.

Selfish people will never get others to trust them, either. You can't trust selfish people any more than you can throw a bull by the tail. They don't keep their word, because they're too focused on doing only what they want to do.

—Paul Petzoldt, founder of the National Outdoor Leadership School

■

Caring Leadership

❏ **Good leaders genuinely care for those they lead.** Good leaders see any trip or event as an opportunity to help people learn and grow.

❏ **Caring leadership is:**

- *putting yourself in others' shoes,* and being sensitive to their needs;
- *being vulnerable.* Putting yourself in another's shoes often means sharing personal experiences of your own;
- *listening.* Nothing demonstrates caring better than active, nonjudgmental listening;
- *putting caring into action.* Intentions are never enough;
- *following through.* Caring is about forming and maintaining relationships, more than one or two wonderful gestures;
- *letting go of judgments.* Caring includes being tolerant of the weaknesses and shortcomings of others;
- *caring for beginners.* Make sure your corrections and instructions to beginners leave them more, not less, confident;
- *correcting with caring.* Try to correct in private, unless there's a general lesson that might benefit others;
- *acknowledging others for their strengths and contributions;* and
- *caring for yourself.* Don't beat yourself up over mistakes—give yourself credit for all the times you do it right.

❏ **Caring is in your interest, too. It's a practical, powerful tool for good leadership.**

- *Caring builds trust.* Trust is a vital link between the leader and those being led. A caring attitude on your part promotes trust in your leadership more than any other factor.
- *Caring provides an early warning system.* Caring helps you be more sensitive early on to behaviors and conditions that can affect the success of your trip.
- *Caring brings people together.* The more team members feel at ease with, and appreciate, each other, the better they'll perform together.
- *Caring can be a powerful tool for dealing with conflict.* It can help defuse anger and fear enough so that both sides can risk the honest dialogue needed to achieve lasting solutions.

Chapter Eight

Taking Responsibility

Taking responsibility is not only about your duties and obligations as a leader. It's about taking full charge of your impact on other people, and about forming fair and positive relationships.

Responsibility—for what? The traditional definition of responsibility focuses on behavior: "do these things; don't do those." It's the definition most of us grew up with.

But it's not enough. To be successful as a leader, you need a broader definition, one that tasks you to be accountable, not just for your behavior, but for your thoughts and feelings as well.

Why? Because you're already constantly affecting the environments in which you live and lead—in the outdoors, at work, in the community, in your home—not only by how you behave, but by how you think and feel. If, for example, you or someone else in your family comes home after a very bad, or a very good, day, the mood of the entire family is affected. Have you ever noticed the power of receptionists to set the mood for an entire office, just by the way they answer the phone? Every city seems to have a few bus drivers who are so good humored that people love to ride their busses. And we have all been on outdoors trips in which one angry person, cursing a broken shoelace or a missing map, manages to set everyone else's teeth on edge.

Your thoughts and feelings, as well as your behavior, affect the world around you. It makes sense to be as responsible as possible for all three, in order to help shape the results you want.

Be conscious of the little things. Part of accepting this broader definition of responsibility is learning to sweat the small stuff. How you answer a sign-up call, introduce newcomers, correct a mistake, and do equipment checks can set a mood that will continue for the entire trip. If you're perceived as being distracted, unfriendly, or belligerent, the trust people put in your leadership will be undermined. If, on the other hand, you handle these incidental encounters with caring, respect, and humor, you'll start to build bonds with your team members that will serve you all well, especially if trouble develops.

Your life is a whole cloth. Another part of this broader definition is taking responsibility for the emotional spillover from one part of your life into another. It's impossible to wall off one part of your life completely from the others, no matter how hard you might try. Leaders who think they can be tense and vicious all week at work and then be relaxed and caring on weekend trips into the mountains are deluding themselves.

Think of the various environments in which you live your life—home, job, community, outdoors—as stage plays, with you helping to write the script for each. In creating each scene, you draw on a personal vocabulary that is shaped by how you're looking at your life at that moment. If that picture is a negative one—for example, you're still fuming over a fight you had with your boss the day before—your vocabulary is going to be weighted with words of anger and frustration, and your script is sure to move the drama in that direction. If, on the other hand, your vocabulary is weighted with words of caring and calm, you'll contribute to quite different outcomes.

Suppose you're leading a group caught out in bad weather, and people are starting to complain.

Ask yourself, first, what your "vocabulary" is at that moment. Are you carrying negative thoughts or feelings into that situation, because, for example, you're cranky from hunger, you hate your job, or you're still mad about something Frank said at the trailhead? If you are, take responsibility for that negative baggage, or it will pop out in body language, cloud your thinking, anger someone else unnecessarily, or in many other ways detract from your ability to lead well.

Acting on positive thoughts and feelings in your vocabulary is as necessary as not acting on negative ones. In the example of that wet and tired group: if a beginner is having a particularly hard time staying dry, go out of your way to offer him some helpful tips; if a grouch insists on taking her frustrations out on you, laugh it off; if everybody else is getting frustrated and tense, dig deep for that sense of humor you know often puts others at ease.

Taking responsibility for your thoughts and feelings, as well as for your behavior, is crucial to good leadership. It will help you develop and maintain positive, trusting relationships with the people you lead. These links are often crucial in a crisis. They will also serve you well that other 98 percent of the time when, absent crises, what's called for are competent, caring responses to the ordinary challenges that accompany any trip or event.

Some effects of being responsible you'll never see—especially those that might spill over from the outdoors into other parts of peoples' lives. For example:

You're leading a winter trip on a beautiful day in the backcountry. The lead members of your group have made a nice ski track through the woods, but Marsha, a beginner who doesn't know any better, tromps through it on her snowshoes. Phil, coming up behind, is furious that the ski track has been ruined and lets Marsha know it in no uncertain terms. The two start yelling at each other.

You intervene, and by patiently listening to them both, telling some stories, and making a few jokes, you quickly and quietly dampen the conflict and help to restore their good moods.

You think nobody sees you talking to the two of them, but Tony's been watching from the other side of a thicket. Tony has a conflict, too—with his teenage son, who has recently been caught shoplifting back in the city. Your caring and patience and humor are exactly what Tony needs to see. Your model will help him deal more effectively with his boy when he gets home—and you'll probably never know this.

Leadership is a contract, and you're responsible for honoring your end of it. Your contract with the group you're leading may not be written, but it is real. People expect you to lead, and, in return, give you the authority to do so.

You're responsible for the following four "clauses" in your contract:
- *maintaining the safety and well-being of your group.* It's up to you more than anybody else to keep people from getting killed, hurt, or lost;
- *helping your group achieve its goal,* whether that entails reaching a summit, running a rapids, or having a fun day in the woods;
- *helping to create a quality experience for the people on the trip;* and
- *meeting the legal requirements of leadership.*

Maintaining the safety and well-being of your group, and helping your group reach its goal. To meet both these responsibilities, you need to prepare well, stay closely attuned to what's happening within the group, and remain alert to factors that could affect the group's safety and/or success. In particular:

- anticipate physical dangers and obstacles, such as those posed by the weather, snow conditions, and stream crossings. See and sense what's going on in your total environment;
- manage the time so that your group is not caught out in an unnecessary bivouac, or a dangerous night descent. Everybody else can lose track of the time if the picture taking from the summit is great, but you must not;
- stay on course. You're responsible, more than anyone else, for preventing your group from getting lost.
- be ready for emergencies. It's your job to make sure the skills and equipment are there for handling accidents, illness, sudden shifts in weather, or other emergencies;
- know how all your people are doing, and the possible effect of their condition on the rest of the group. If Tim's exhausted, he's much more likely to fall; if Claudia's blister gets any worse, she'll never make the last two steep miles to the lake;
- know where all your people are. If you're leading from the front or rear of your group, make sure you have a competent person at the other end.

Helping to create a quality experience. Good leaders take responsibility for more than keeping followers safe and directing them toward their goals. They also take responsibility for helping make the quality of experience as high as possible for the people they lead. While there are certainly limits to how much a leader can do, or should try to do, to make a trip "fun," basic responsibilities include:

- helping to build and maintain positive personal relationships within your team. Model the caring approaches described in Chapter Seven to help bring the people on your team together. And if there's conflict, or if one or two difficult people threaten to undermine the good mood within your group, use the suggestions in Chapter Twelve to defuse the situation and find cooperative solutions.
- being a coach as well as a leader. Try to find ways to let everyone test and improve their abilities and skills. Within the bounds of common sense, don't impose safety standards so stringent that all physical challenges become trivial. Let your people "go for it." Give them opportunities to challenge themselves.

If you know some helpful techniques, then demonstrate them along the way. Show Justin how he'll be more comfortable with his pack higher up on his back; demonstrate to Allison an easier way of tying into her belay; suggest to Andy a better choice of waxes for his skis.

■ sharing your knowledge of nature. Of course, you need to sense how much of this kind of sharing is appropriate in each circumstance. But it's often a gift to team members if—assuming you have this knowledge— you take the time to point out edible plants, comment on the geology, or interpret animal tracks. Ask others to share their lore, too.

■ not ignoring aesthetic delights for the sake of making good time. Given no time crunch, stop to smell the flowers. I remember once being on a training climb on Mount Rainier with a team bound for Mount Everest. It was late August, the time of peak wildflower color in Paradise Valley, which begins just below the climbing route and stretches all the way down to the road. That team came off the glacier and charged down the valley practically at the run, looking neither right nor left at what is one of the most spectacular mountain scenes in the world. You could hardly hear the whistles of the marmots over the clank of their climbing hardware. I hope they had a good time in the Himalayas.

■

In the mountains of the Soviet Caucasus, a member of our climbing team decided he wasn't having a good time and that he wanted to go home even though our itinerary had several weeks to run. He appealed to the Soviet officials to change his travel arrangements, but they gave him the big *nyet*. He was stuck, he was angry, and he wanted to know what Scott Fischer, the expedition leader, was going to do about it.

"Well, buddy," Scott told him, "you're either cruisin' or you're bummin'. It's up to you which it's going to be, but I'll let you in on a little secret—cruisin's a whole lot more fun."

Outdoor leaders do accept the responsibility to ensure, as much as possible, the safety of those they lead, and to make the hard choices about when to go forward and when to turn back. Beyond that, leaders can inspire, teach, entertain, and in many other ways shape the framework upon which an adventure can unfold.

Within that framework, however, group members must bear much of the responsibility for the quality of their own experience. Leaders offer opportunities, but then it is up to those they are leading to make of those opportunities what they will. The choice of having a fantastic experience instead of a disappointing failure is often a matter of perception, both at the moment it is occurring and in hindsight, but the choice is definitely there for each group member to make.

In reviewing decisions they made during a trip, people new to outdoor leadership are often hard on themselves, taking too much blame for any dissatisfaction among group members. While successful outings do involve an intricate dance between leaders and group members, each person bears responsibility for the degree of optimism or pessimism he or she is willing to invest in the adventure. Each person ultimately determines whether to engage in events from a standpoint that is essentially positive, negative, or somewhere in between.

The fellow in the Caucasus who couldn't go home insisted on staying grumpy, bummin' in base camp day after day rather than hitting the heights. I would argue that he made the wrong choice, but it was his choice to make, not mine. As for me, I'll have to agree with Scott that cruisin' is always the better way to go.

—Robert Birkby, backcountry trail crew foreman
and author of the *Boy Scout Handbook,* 10th edition

■

Meeting the legal requirements of leadership. America is by far the most litigious society in the world, with more lawyers per capita than anyplace else. Whatever you think of this, the fact is that the threat of lawsuits and the cost of liability insurance have become daunting obstacles for nearly every organization that offers a public service, from schools to doctors' offices—to outdoors organizations.

Maintaining superb quality control over the courses and trips you lead is, unfortunately, not enough. No matter how professional and polished you are, you and your organization can still get sued by people who are disgruntled, unrealistic, mercenary—or a combination of the three. And the costs of a legal defense can be enormous.

If you've been designated a leader by an organization, make sure you're protected by a legally sound waiver policy, and that all the people on your trip have signed waivers that formally absolve both you and the organization in case of death or injury. Using waivers is also an excellent idea if you're organizing and leading trips on your own, with groups that include people other than your family and friends.

Personally, I hate the concept of waivers because it undermines the feeling of informal, shared responsibility that should govern every outdoors trip and obscures the fact that accepting some personal risk is, or should be, part of any trip into the outdoors. Had any of my college climbing buddies or I broken a leg learning to rock climb many years ago, suing our climbing club would have been unthinkable. Times have changed.

What constitutes a legally sound waiver varies somewhat from state to state, but they all share common elements. Any waiver form should contain clear language indicating that the party signing the agreement is assuming all risk of injury or damage resulting from the activity which he or she is about to join. Specific risks that can be anticipated should be item-ized and key elements should be printed in boldface type or in some other manner that makes them stand out on the page. The party signing must be given a reasonable opportunity to read and understand the document.*

Waivers, no matter how skillfully written, don't always hold up in court. You as leader, and your organization, can still be held liable for injury if:

- you're guilty of "gross negligence," usually defined by law as "an act falling greatly below the standard established by law for the protection of others against unreasonable risk of harm." The courts fight over this one, but a common-sense interpretation on your part should keep you out of trouble. Don't do anything ille-gal, for example. Don't do anything outrageously stupid, either, such as camping in an avalanche chute, heading into the bush without a compass and map, or crossing a crevassed glacier with-out a rope.
- you take your group beyond the anticipated activities of that trip and expose trip members to risks not specifically known and ap-preciated in advance. For example, if you're leading a trip adver-tised as a day hike, don't take people up a rock climb instead.

If a person on a trip you're leading insists on separating him- or her-self from your group in order to do something you regard as unwise, for-mally register your opposition in front of a witness.

Don't abuse leadership roles. It's sometimes tempting to let your responsibility for leadership go to your head. Make sure you don't use your position as leader to justify rude, crude, or high-handed behavior you'd never think of using if you weren't in charge. This applies not only to club trips for which the organization has appointed you leader but also to informal leadership roles taken on, for example, when you're out with less experienced friends who look to you for guidance.

At a more subtle level, don't use the authority of a leadership role to avoid having to deal fairly and sensitively with those you lead. Suppose you've made a route-finding decision you're not sure about and someone on your team challenges it. Don't stand on your authority for the sole purpose of getting your way. Take in the new information and be willing to change course if you're persuaded that the new direction is better.

The responsibilities of following. Even as a trained leader, there will be times when you're on trips led by others. Remember your role as fol-lower. Give your leaders the respect they need to do their jobs, *especially* those with less experience. Nothing is more annoying to a new leader than to have a more experienced person along on the trip who adopts an aloof,

---

* See, for example, "Assumption of Risk Under Washington Law," Charles Van Gorder, *Washington State Bar News*, October 1995.

judgmental, or condescending attitude. Second-guess your leader's decisions only if absolutely necessary to prevent a bad situation, and then try to do so in private, not before the rest of the group.

In a positive vein, support the leader in any way you can—for example, by contributing to the morale of the group, by pitching in to help as a member of the team, and by generally serving as a model for the supportive "followership" you appreciate when you are in charge.

Even if you rarely expect to lead, don't let that stop you from learning and occasionally testing leadership skills. Think of it as you would a CPR course: the information is good to know even if you hope you'll never have to use it. In addition, when you understand and experience the pressures and responsibilities of leadership, you'll be more understanding and effective in a supporting role. Having once put yourself in a leader's shoes, you'll more easily appreciate the risks and challenges they're taking on.

Taking Responsibility

❑ **Responsibility—for what?** It's not just your behavior that counts but your thoughts and feelings as well.
- *Be conscious of the little things.*
- *Your life is a whole cloth.* Take responsibility for any emotional spill-over between your personal life and your leadership roles.

❑ **Some effects of being responsible you'll never see,** especially those that spill over from the outdoors into other parts of peoples' lives.

❑ **Leadership is a contract.** You're responsible for:
- *maintaining the safety and well-being of your group, and helping the group reach its goal.*
  - Anticipate physical dangers and obstacles.
  - Manage the time.
  - Stay on course.
  - Be ready for emergencies.
  - Know how all your people are doing.
  - Know where all your people are.
- *helping to create a quality experience for the people on the trip.*
  - Help to build and maintain positive personal relationships within your team.
  - Be a coach as well as a leader.
  - Share your knowledge of nature.
  - Don't ignore aesthetic delights.
- *meeting the legal requirements of leadership.* Make sure your outdoors organization has a legally sound waiver policy. Be aware that waivers may not stand up if you do anything that is considered grossly negligent or take your group beyond anticipated activities for that trip.

❑ **Don't abuse leadership roles.** Don't use your position to justify negative behavior you'd never think of using if you weren't in charge, or to avoid having to deal with those you lead with fairness and sensitivity.

❑ **The responsibilities of following.** If, as a leader, you find yourself in a follower role, give your leaders the respect they need to do their jobs, especially if the leader has less experience than you do.

Chapter Nine

Communicating Effectively

Good communication is not simply a matter of getting your facts straight and delivering them accurately. It's also about common sense, about being aware of your environment, and about being willing to take enough responsibility for your impact on people's lives.

Learning to communicate may start when we're infants, but mastering the skill is a lifetime challenge. Think of all the snafus you've experienced at home, at work, or in the outdoors, and ask yourself how many of them occurred because some vital communication was incorrect, garbled, misunderstood—or perhaps wasn't even made at all.

Communications skills are particularly valuable when you're a leader, and your decisions, information, suggestions, and encouragement must get to the people in your group.

To succeed, start with good information, then get it to the people who need to know it—accurately, completely, and on time. Double-check that your message got through—as you sent it. Keep your communications as personal and open as possible, and learn to tailor them so they'll get through to people from widely different backgrounds. Watch for inconsistencies between the content of your message and your body language and tone of voice. Remember that good communication is a two-way street: you also have to be a good listener, which includes soliciting and paying attention to feedback on your performance. Finally, if you have to give a public presentation, it needn't be scary; the core requirement is to know both your subject and your audience.

Make sure your communications are both complete and accurate. You're leading a trip and need to convey information about equipment and schedules to the people who've signed up; you're chairing a committee and must make sure that other members know the background of a problem to be discussed; or you're sending a letter or email to a county official objecting to new clearcuts, and must answer all the opposing arguments.

The initial requirement in all these situations is the same: to assemble information that is both complete and accurate. Before you pick up the phone or pen or turn on your computer, put yourself in the shoes of your listeners or readers. What do they need to know? Then make a list of the points you need to make.

Check your information for accuracy; do whatever additional research may be necessary using the web and other sources. If there's time, have a colleague check your work. Are you sure the logging road past Whistler Creek is still open after the fire? Is Tuesday the deadline for the newspaper notice? Didn't someone tell you the phone number of the Darrington Ranger Station had recently changed?

Needless to say, if you discover any holes in your information fill them in before you make the calls or send the letters or emails.

Target the information to the people who need to know it. Once you're sure your information is as complete and accurate as possible, the next link in the chain is to target those who need it.

Everyone going on your trip or helping plan your event needs to know the basic details of schedules, equipment, routes, and other such data. But certain people need extra information. Those driving need to know that chains are required on the Mount Baker Highway this time of year. The chair of your media committee must have the name of the local editor. The fellow who had bypass surgery last year needs more detailed knowledge concerning the physical demands of your route. The person buying groceries has to know how many vegetarians are signed up for the trip. Yes, this is all basic, but think it through. The last thing you need is the guy with all the tents going up the wrong road because he didn't get word about the change in route.

■

Communication on a trip needs to be a constant, two-way process. On Everest in 1984, we were struggling through waist-deep snow up to the North Col, without oxygen, at 22,000 feet. There were plenty of signals that there was avalanche danger, and I could see fracture joints. I was breaking trail at that point, and I finally stopped and said to the rest of the team, "I think it's getting a little spooky. I don't like the looks of this." John Roskelley was behind me, and the first thing he said was, "Lou, I'm glad you said it first. I've been feeling the same way!"

The lesson was that we all should have been sharing our concerns from the beginning. We turned around just 400 feet short of the North Col and it delayed our climb for two weeks. But there were avalanches all that afternoon.

—Lou Whittaker, climber/guide, President, Rainier Mountaineering Inc., and author of *Lou Whittaker: Memoirs of a Mountain Guide*

■

Choose the right means for sending your message. Be as personal as time and resources allow. A handwritten note or letter or a printed letter with an added handwritten line or two, will catch people's attention better than an email. A face-to-face meeting is better than a telephone conversation or a texted message, but a voice-to-voice phone conversation is better than dueling answering machines.

Back up oral communications with written or email reminders, if the message is in any detail. It's a good idea, for example, to mail a road map and/or email directions to anyone not familiar with the trailhead location. Include a list of equipment needed for the trip. If you're giving a lecture or leading a training course, back up your oral presentation and instructions with handouts containing key points.

Get the message there on time. Expectations and requirements that demand long response times need to be communicated well in advance. If you want the members of your team to carry avalanche rescue beacons, many of them will need time to procure them. If you know there's a moderate possibility of a bivouac on your trip, people will need to adjust work and family schedules to permit a day's delay. If there's one difficult move on an otherwise easy climb, make sure the least proficient climbers know about it early so they can either prepare themselves for the challenge or take another trip.

Confirm that your message got through as you intended it. The best information in the world will not be of much use if it doesn't get through, or if it's garbled in transmission.

Take the simple, shouted signals new rock climbers learn their first day on the cliff. The signals are crucial, designed to prevent possible fatal misunderstandings about who's climbing and who's holding the rope. But even using simple signals such as these can be easier said than done—a lesson I learned many years ago.

_____

A couple of months after my first rock climbing lesson I decided— being a young tiger—to tackle Shockley's Ceiling, a formidable climb on the Shawangunks Cliffs in the Hudson River Valley. The crucial move involved hanging by one's hands from an overhang 200 feet above ground, then doing a pull-up to a ledge above. My friend Bill, leading the climb, scampered over the ceiling as if he were doing chin-ups in a gym. Then it was my turn.

A stiff breeze had come up and I couldn't see Bill, hidden by the overhang. Did I hear a shouted signal that it was safe for me to climb—or not? I couldn't be sure. Perhaps it was a climber on a nearby route. Perhaps it was the wind. I waited. Then the rope jerked sharply. Had Bill slipped, even on the easy part above the ceiling? Or had he stopped, tied himself to the cliff, and now was trying to signal through the rope that I should start up? Had we discussed rope tugs as backup signals? If we had, I couldn't remember which was which. Were two tugs a signal to climb—or three? Understanding that I couldn't stay on that small ledge forever, after ten minutes I unclipped from the piton that was securing me to the cliff and started up. I hung by my hands from that overhang, without being sure Bill had secured the climbing rope above me. It was one of those giddy moments that only a nineteen-year-old could savor. Only after I'd made the move and felt Bill pull in the slack was I sure I'd made the right choice.

But it's not too often we can blame rock walls and wind for miscommunications. Human error is much more likely. Ann thinks Cathy told everyone about the new meeting place—but Cathy thought Ann was doing the telling. Tom typed "not" in the meeting announcement when he meant to type "now." Ed's Canadian friend gives distances in kilometers but Ed hears miles.

There are as many ways to garble communications as there are people. If you doubt that, remember the parlor game in which Person #1 whispers a short message to Person #2 who whispers it to Person #3, and so on. By the time the message gets back to Person #1, it's often nothing at all like the original.

Double-check that your message got through—as you intended it. If you're even a little unsure, make a spot call or two to confirm.

If you've just delivered a complex message over the phone, ask the person on the other end to read the message back. This may seem awkward, but risking a little embarrassment now is better than experiencing a major foul-up later on.

And if you suspect that physical circumstances, such as a howling wind, might make any communications difficult, then discuss and practice a backup signaling system in advance.

Sometimes the danger is not that the message won't get through clearly and completely, but that it will be misinterpreted at the receiving end. Trip and climb descriptions are classic examples. "Moderately difficult," for example, has an entirely different meaning for an experienced climber than for a beginner. If you have any question about how to interpret key phrases in guidebooks, such as "can be done in six hours," "moderately steep," or "easily fordable," check alternate sources. Do your best to clear up the ambiguities before setting foot on the trail.

Don't send mixed messages. Watch for inconsistencies between the content of your words and your tone of voice and body language.

Who said English isn't a tonal language? Take Andy, a pleasant if somewhat clumsy fellow who doesn't realize he's slowing up the entire group. When he catches up at one point, he gulps his breath and then asks you, "How'm I doing?" You can:

- understand that he's doing his best, and to encourage him, smile and reply with a cheery "You're doing just fine";
- resign yourself to his incompetence and mumble, "You're doing just fine" in a low monotone, almost under your breath;
- seethe with anger and turn on him with a cynical "You're doing *just* fine."

The words are the same. The messages are totally different.

Body language can contribute to making the message even more mixed if only because it's so often unconscious. We've all heard people make optimistic statements about health, money, a relationship, or any other goal while their face muscles sagged in despair and their voices grew tired and faint. "We're sure grandfather will be well soon." "We're confident that fourth-quarter earnings will be better." "I know she will come back to me." "I'm sure the summit is just over the next rise."

Anger is another message people often think they're hiding—but aren't. Phil arrives at the trip carpool point still steaming over a fight he had with his wife. You know him well, so you say, "Phil, you seem upset; want to talk about it?" Phil says, "No, no, I'm OK," while the veins on his neck are bulging, his color is that of a tomato, and he looks as if he's ready to put his fist through the wall of his camper.

Then there's Alice, the leader who's completely accessible—or so she says. Twice you've suggested that the slope she's heading for might be dangerously unstable. She seems to be ignoring everything you say, and finally you ask her why. Somehow you don't believe her when she smiles at you and says, "Why, I'm not ignoring you; on the contrary, I'm listening to everything you say." Maybe she's not credible because her arms are crossed tightly in front of her chest and her eyes flash "shark" instead of "friend."

As a way of becoming more conscious of your own body language, try this exercise in the mirror, or with a friend. Compose a message with a strong emotional content, then deliver it with body language that conveys the exact opposite meaning. Overdo it. By exaggerating the mistake in practice, you'll gain insights into how to avoid making it in a real situation. You'll also be more likely to notice if you do slip up. And you'll certainly be more aware of mixed messages from body language when you see them in others.

Keep your communications user-friendly. Unless you're handling a dire emergency and have no time for anything but shouted orders, keep your communications with team members as personal and open as possible. Encourage others to follow your lead. The more personal and open all the communications are within your group, the more comfortable with each other people will be—a valuable asset, especially if your team gets into trouble.

Take responsibility for the effect of your communications on each person—especially if your audiences include men and women of different ages and backgrounds. No two people are the same. Yelling a good-natured "Hey, Nathan, move your butt!" may be a completely appropriate communication to a seventeen-year-old boy, but I suggest being careful using that kind of language with anybody else. A handwritten note scrawled on a yellow pad is fine if you're reminding a buddy to bring his extra tent. But it would be the wrong vehicle for asking your landlord to extend the clubhouse lease.

These examples are easy. But now fine-tune the advice. Does anyone in your group have sensitivities that might need special handling—for example, political or religious beliefs that might require more than average care in choosing language? Are there any non-native speakers who will not get your jokes and puns? Who on the team needs directions repeated three times? Who tends to charge off before hearing them even once? The better you get to know your people as individuals, the more effectively you'll be able to communicate with each one.

Taking the time and making the effort to tailor your communications to specific individuals in your group is about more than merely getting the message through. It's about taking full responsibility as a leader for your impact on other human beings who, at least for a time, are looking to you for guidance. Honoring this responsibility is not an extreme demand, but a measure of your caring for people and the quality of experience they have when they're with you. It's an essential quality of good leadership.

Be a good listener.
- Value the opinions of others even when you don't accept them.
- Go out of your way to create and maintain dialogue with those you lead. Practically speaking, this means checking in regularly

with each member of your group, and, especially if you sense a problem, not being satisfied with a perfunctory response. The exchange: "How're you doing?" "Oh, fine" is a social form, not a useful communication. There's no need to be oversolicitous or nosy, but good leaders are truly interested in what is going on with the members of the group.

Solicit feedback. Encouraging feedback on your own performance is a vital way for you to learn and grow as a leader. The best way to obtain honest and direct feedback is to ask for it, and to explain why you're asking. Your team members will respect you for making the request, and most often will respond constructively.

Evaluate feedback carefully. Pay more attention to consistent patterns than to isolated comments. If any comments are shockers, check them out by sharing them with others who know you well.

■

I've been guiding outdoors adventures for twenty-one years, and of all the "people-type" problems I've seen, 99 percent were caused by breakdowns in communication.

Communicating means including your whole group in the decision-making process, as far as you possibly can. If people feel that their views were at least considered—even if in the end they weren't accepted—it can make a big difference in their attitudes. Given the time, explain your decisions, especially if the rationale is not evident. For example, if you turn back on a sunny day because you know that an innocent-looking slope ahead could avalanche, you'll avoid a lot of trouble if you carefully explain your reasons to the beginner who doesn't know or see what you do.

—Peter Whittaker, climber/guide, Summits Adventure Travel

■

MAKING PUBLIC PRESENTATIONS

I know outdoors leaders who'd rather climb up a vertical cliff without a rope than give a speech or other public presentation. But there are definitely times when the responsibilities of outdoor leadership include teaching courses, chairing committees, or making presentations. The longer you stay active as a leader, the more likely you are to be called on to make public presentations of some kind.

Speaking in public doesn't have to be scary. The core advice is to know both your subject and your audience. A written outline is a good idea, but your personal manner as a speaker is more important. Stay flexible, spontaneous, and informal—don't be afraid to express your feelings. Show that you care for the people to whom you're speaking. Tell stories, and invite your audience to participate, if possible. While your role is to convey information, you can also empower people as learners.

Prepare well.

- Do your research; know your subject matter.
- Find out, in advance, to whom you're talking. Is there an experience, attitude, or ideology that most of them share? What levels of competence and knowledge do they already have? Your presentation should be neither too basic nor too advanced.
- Make a written outline of what you want to say. Most presentations follow a rough form that answers the following questions, more or less in this order:
  - Who am I?
  - What is the issue/problem/challenge to be discussed, and why should this audience care about it?
  - What are my ideas regarding this issue?
  - Why do I think my ideas will work?
  - What, if anything, do I want my audience to do?

Make introductions. Start by introducing yourself. If the group is small enough, ask the people in your audience to introduce themselves as well. Ask them to say not only their names, but also a few words about their backgrounds and their expectations for the session. By breaking the ice quickly, you'll create a comfortable atmosphere in which everybody will be more receptive to what you have to say.

Be flexible. The best presentations always have some spontaneity about them. Unless absolutely necessary, avoid sticking rigidly to a plan or outline when circumstances are pushing you to bend. For example:

You're on a forest walk giving a lecture on edible plants, and a nine-year-old interrupts with a question about mushrooms. You could ask him to wait until you get to the mushrooms portion of your talk, but this would risk deflating his enthusiasm and curiosity—and making everybody else hesitant to interrupt, too. Or you might understand that interrupting your lesson plan to give him at least a preliminary answer would be not only a useful addition to the talk, but also make your presentation more informal and accessible for the entire group.

Be "human-centered."

- Keep your style and language informal.
- Tell plenty of stories, especially personal ones, to illustrate your points.
- Minimize or eliminate the use of Powerpoint text slides; they re-

duce personal contact with your audience.

- Be genuinely interested in the concerns and questions people raise.
- Make your presentations as participatory as time and circumstance allow.
- Don't be shy about expressing your feelings, or about evoking the feelings of people in your audience. For example:

You're trying to convince your club to devote time and money to repairing the fire lookout on Big Bear Mountain. Members will certainly want to hear about budgets, required permits, schedules, and all other details. But they're unlikely to be swayed unless you reach their hearts as well as their heads. Describe the challenge in exciting terms. Draw a picture of the completed project that is clear and compelling. Get your audience to share the enthusiasm you feel.

Provide a summary. Hearing a presentation is not the same as reading a book or magazine; listeners can't go back and look up a point they missed. So, especially in a longer presentation, tell your audience what your main points are soon after you start, and then remind them about these points shortly before you end. If there are numerous points and/or technical data, it's also a good idea to hand out a written outline.

Empower people as learners. Never talk down to an audience based on your "superior" knowledge. The challenge is not to have them anoint you as an authority but to excite them with the knowledge you're sharing. Unless your presentation is about techniques that must be done precisely, such as administering CPR or rigging a rappel, don't worry about nailing down every angle in the first pass. In fact, it's often a good idea to leave time and space for people to wonder, to ponder the unknowns, and then to ask questions.

Empower yourself as a teacher. Honor the importance of what you're doing. For some of your audience, your presentation will be the only opportunity they will have to learn about your subject. For others, your presentation may so excite them that they'll pursue the subject further on their own.

Public presentations, as with any other form of leader communications, call for organization and attention to detail. Often, however, the key requirement for a successful presentation is your own capacity to care for others and to be responsible for your effect on them. Establish links to your audiences at that human level. Give of yourself. Transmit not only your information, but the message that you are not just teacher but friend.

Communicating Effectively

❑ **Make sure your communications are both accurate and complete.** Put yourself in the shoes of your listeners or readers. What do they need to know?

❑ **Target the information to the people who need it.**

❑ **Choose the right means for sending your message.** The more personal the means, the faster it will get the receiver's attention. Back up oral communications with written or email reminders.

❑ **Get the message there on time.** Expectations and requirements that demand long response times need to be communicated well in advance.

❑ **Confirm that your message got through as you intended it.** Make spot calls to double-check. Have complex messages read back to you. Develop backup signaling systems if necessary. Clear up any ambiguities in language before they can do harm.

❑ **Don't send mixed messages.** Watch for inconsistencies in the content of your words and your tone of voice and body language.

❑ **Keep your communications with team members user-friendly,** as personal and open as possible. Encourage others to follow your lead.

❑ **Take responsibility for the effect of your communications on each person,** especially if your audiences include men and women of different ages and backgrounds.

❑ **Be a good listener.** Value the opinions of others even when you don't accept them. Go out of your way to create and maintain dialogue with those you lead.

❑ **Solicit feedback** on your own performance.

Making Public Presentations

❏ **Prepare well.**
  - *Do your research; know your subject.*
  - *Find out, in advance, to whom you're talking.*
  - *Make a written outline of what you want to say.*

❏ **Make introductions.** Start by intoducing yourself and, if the group is small enough, ask the people in your audience to introduce themselves as well.

❏ **Be flexible.** The best presentations always have some spontaneity about them.

❏ **Be "human-centered."**
  - *Keep your style and language informal.*
  - *Tell plenty of stories, especially personal ones.*
  - *Minimize or eliminate the use of Powerpoint text slides.*
  - *Be genuinely interested in the concerns and questions people raise.*
  - *Make your presentations as participatory as time and circumstance allow.*
  - *Don't be shy about expressing your feelings, or about evoking the feelings of people in your audience.*

❏ **Provide a summary.**

❏ **Empower people as learners.** Excite them with the knowledge you're sharing.

❏ **Empower yourself as a teacher.** Honor the importance of what you're doing.

Chapter Ten

Courage

People who are good at taking risks continually seek out and find meaning in what tests them. They embark on risky activities knowing that what they are doing makes sense to them at a very deep level of their being.

Courage counts. In our culture, courage is the guiding theme in the sagas and myths that embellish our past and inspire us to excel. Courage is the key quality we admire in the men and women we call our heroes.

At a more personal level, courage is what keeps you as leader in the game, functioning effectively in the face of dangers and risks. Chapter Two described the importance of creating a strong personal vision of yourself-as-leader. Nothing adds more to that self-image than knowing you have the courage to deal with whatever comes your way. It's this confidence that helps you dig deep for inner calm, then square your shoulders and act.

■

I think it's important to value risk. Good leaders have a curiosity about life, and about what they can do with it. They like challenges. If you don't risk, nothing will happen in your life. There's no security in nature, so why should there be security in life? Everything is risky. I say, "Warm both hands before the fires of life."

It's a lot easier to be brave if you take things one day at a time, or even one hour at a time. Don't project out all the tough stuff so that it looks overwhelming.

I also think of my heroes and models—people like Willi Unsoeld. I remind myself that the human spirit is incredible. I'm involved in taking

people who are blind and deaf and handicapped in other ways up mountains. I see what they can do, and it inspires me.
—Lou Whittaker, climber/guide, President, Rainier Mountaineering Inc.,
and author of *Lou Whittaker: Memoirs of a Mountain Guide*

■

What is courage? What constitutes a courageous act for me might be ho-hum for you. What scares a five-year-old might not scare an adult.

If you're asked to name courageous people, who first comes to mind? firefighters rushing into a burning building? soldiers facing death to save the lives of their buddies? the police patrolling a drug-infested neighborhood? daredevils such as high-wire acrobats, stuntpeople, and mountain climbers?

If images such as these—courage in the face of physical danger—are what first comes to mind, you're not alone. For most people—perhaps especially for those of us who seek adventure in the outdoors—braving physical danger is a major model for courage.

For the whole first part of my life, I defined courage in this very physical way. I took a lot of risks, nearly all of them physical: I crawled up steep cliffs of ice and rock, dodged bullets from Algerian terrorists and Viet Cong guerrillas, and dealt with thugs and mercenaries and warlords in far-off places. Taking on physical dangers became a way of life, and I got very good at it.

But sometime in my thirties, by fits and starts, I began to put physical adventure and risk taking into the deeper perspective of what my life was about. I began to deal with challenges of personal meaning and relationships that I had been avoiding for years. As I pursued this path, it soon became apparent that the physical dangers that had all but consumed my life until then were the easy risks, especially for a strong, young male.

The hard risks—the ones that really scared me—tested my spirit, not my body. They included:

- admitting and learning from mistakes;
- trying something new and persisting, despite the fear of failing;
- forming relationships;
- dealing with conflict calmly and compassionately, when the temptation was to rage;
- standing up for an unpopular idea I believed was right, even when I knew I would lose friends, money, or stature.

Risks such as these then seemed to be coming at me from all directions. Of course, I thought each one was my own unique agony. Since then I've learned differently. These risks, the ones that test the spirit, challenge most of us far more frequently than do physical risks, even in outdoor leadership situations—which leads to this definition: *Courage is facing what scares you, including risks that test your spirit as well as your body.*

Courage is not about being free from fear. Only a fool is fearless. Courage is the ability to do the right thing, and do it well, even when you *are* afraid.

The amount of courage you need to cope with any situation depends on the risks you perceive. If the risks you perceive are small, then a little straightening of the shoulders ought to do. But if you're scared out of your wits, the amount of courage needed to cope might be overwhelming. This suggests two basic strategies for dealing with situations that scare you: you can reduce the perceived risks; and/or you can summon up the necessary courage to deal with them.

Being courageous starts with you as an individual. For me, a big part of it is simply remembering where I've been. As a kid, I had a lot of adventures. And as a climber, leader, and guide, I've been involved in lots of dangerous situations, and some in which people have died, including a 1981 avalanche on Mount Rainier that killed eleven people, but spared me. I've seen it as bad as it gets. I know there are times when you're going to be exposed, and that for the next two minutes or twenty minutes, it's a role of the dice.

When people want to know why I act the way I do in a dangerous or potentially dangerous situation, I wish I could play back for them a tape of all the accidents I've seen and how much danger I've faced. Part of my courage is having a lot of respect for what's out there and a good understanding of how bad things can get.

Never let fear build. Never just sit there and imagine all the worst scenarios. All you're doing then is making things worse than they actually are.

—Peter Whittaker, climber/guide, Summits Adventure Travel

Reduce the perceived risks by increasing control. The biggest risks are almost always situations in which you must face forces that are unknown or perceived to be beyond your control. An effective way to reduce perceived risks is to increase the degree of control you have in tight situations. You can do this by:

- increasing your knowledge;
- acquiring the right tools;
- gaining experience; and
- getting help.

The following example illustrates how all four of these factors can help you increase your control over a dangerous situation—and reduce your perceived risk:

Sally has been leading outdoors trips for years, but she has never had to deal with a major accident—until today. A beginner puts his weight on a loose rock and takes a bad fall down a scree slope covered with sharp slate. When Sally and the rest of her team reach him, he's bleeding from a dozen cuts, two of them serious, and has a compound fracture of his left leg. The person Sally thought would be her best first-aider sees all the blood and faints. Someone else starts to panic. Sally has only seconds to organize and apply the first aid. Then she has to organize her team to get the injured person off that dangerous slope and to a hospital as soon as possible. She also has to get full control of herself, and be able to communicate calmness and confidence even though she can feel the fear standing like little needles on the back of her neck.

Sally can reduce the risks she perceives by increasing her sense of control over this difficult situation. She needs to take a deep breath and then remind herself that she finished a Red Cross refresher course only last fall, that her team has plenty of first aid supplies, and that she's had years of training and experience in leading. She also gains control knowing that once the victim is stabilized, she can send one of the stronger hikers back to the road for help, which hopefully will arrive before nightfall.

The situation Sally faces is serious enough, but far less so than if she and her pals had wandered into the mountains without training, experience, the proper equipment, or the means and knowledge to get help—and then faced a serious injury.

Under these kinds of circumstances, without benefit of the factors that reduce perceived risk, many people experience a *loss* of control. They describe their situation as "being blindsided by events," or "bad luck." Their level of fear rises, which makes them feel—quite accurately—even less in control, and so a vicious downward spiral begins. Their perceived risk escalates as their sense of control plummets. They panic. This is what happens, for example, in cases of lost hikers feeling so frantic that they actually stumble across roads and keep right on going into the bush on the other side.

Dealing with panic. If you're ever in a situation in which someone on your team begins to panic, focus your efforts on helping that person calm down enough so that he can recognize and use the control he still has over the threatening situation.

- Make clear your genuine concern. ("I know you're scared.")
- Speak clearly, calmly, and honestly about the situation and your strategy for improving it. Never lie. ("Don't worry, avalanches never occur twice in the same place.")
- Describe in detail the next steps to be taken. Frightened people are more scared of the unknown than the known dangers, and they find great comfort in the specifics of the answers to their fears.
- If there's time, tell stories about times when you were scared but still managed to cope.
- Maintain your sense of humor. A well-timed joke often helps.

■

My friend Dan, a mountaineer of some renown, told me about walking barefoot through fire. It focused his attention and cleared his mind, he said, and I should try it, too.

I told him he was nuts. I had no intention of shuffling through red-hot embers, though I did agree to go to the woods with him just to watch.

The logs were piled as high as my shoulder, and it took several hours for them to burn down enough for Dan to rake the coals into a deep, glowing bed a dozen feet long. Wiggling his bare toes, he studied the fire a moment and then simply walked across, leaving dark footprints in the embers.

The effect was electrifying. The survival instinct hardwired into my brain screamed that people can't step into a fire and remain unscathed, but I had just witnessed someone doing exactly that. I yanked off my shoes and walked over the coals, feeling their brittle texture but, amazingly, none of their heat.

"Once you see it for what it is, you know it can be done," Dan said when I reached the other side. "The fear is just smoke and mirrors."

I often think of that night, especially when I am in the backcountry with a crew. There is the obvious context of leading through example by simply showing that something is doable. But more to the point is the matter of courage.

As outdoor leaders, we all eventually find ourselves in difficulties where we must act in spite of our own fear and that of the people we are leading. If we can see a situation for what it is and nothing more—a storm, an avalanche, a fractured leg, a lost hiker—solutions are likely to present themselves. Those solutions may be extremely challenging, but at least we will know in which direction to start.

A key to leadership in dangerous times lies not in having every answer, but rather in seeing through the smoke and mirrors and, in spite of our misgivings, taking the first steps. That is the beginning of courage, a concept every bit as elusive as footprints in the fire and, once you have seen it, every bit as possible.

—Robert Birkby, backcountry trail crew foreman and author of the *Boy Scout Handbook*, 10th edition

■

Preparing for next time. No matter how well you handled the last crisis, look for ways you can strengthen the factors that will help you feel even more in control next time. Take more training courses and ask other experienced leaders how they would have handled your situation; acquire better or more equipment if needed; and explore additional avenues for getting help, perhaps by contacting nearby ranger stations or search and rescue units.

Find courage by finding meaning. The strategy of reducing perceived risks by increasing your control over a dangerous situation will take you only so far. Perceived risks can never be brought to zero. You're still going to be facing danger. You're still going to get scared.

The second strategy for dealing with dangerous situations is to increase the amount of courage you have for dealing with them.

What I discovered—as I struggled to be as brave in my spirit as I was in the world of physical adventure—was that people who were good at taking risks, whether in cities or on mountains, focused on the personal *meaning* their risky activities had for them. They saw the risks as integral parts of a path they already knew was meaningful, therefore a path they felt very good about and were committed to taking. The risks didn't go away, but seen in this broader context they became more like speed bumps than ten-foot walls. They seemed more worth taking and these risk-takers became more willing and confident to take them. To put it another way—the commitment these people already had for walking a meaningful path spilled over onto the risks they faced along the way, and they were better motivated to act in the face of fear. It can be like this for anyone.

———————

Consider Lois Gibbs. As a young housewife and mother, she and other residents of Love Canal learned that their homes were built on a toxic waste dump. Suddenly, everything she loved, everything that meant something to her, starting with her children, was in danger. Gibbs began to fight. She was initially so scared that she quit her first neighborhood campaign after knocking on one door. Reminding herself of what was at stake, she eventually spearheaded a massive effort that helped to relocate all the residents of Love Canal. She didn't stop with her first victory but went on to found Citizens' Clearinghouse for Hazardous Waste to help other toxin-plagued communities.

Lois Gibbs became a national figure and a political powerhouse in the environmental movement. Keeping people safe from toxic wastes was profoundly important to her and focusing on that meaning gave her the courage she needed.

For me in my thirties, this increasingly obvious link between the meaning people like Lois Gibbs found in the challenges they faced and the courage they demonstrated in dealing with them, provided the guidance I needed. At last I saw a path for developing the courage I needed for taking the risks that were then testing my spirit, and limiting both my personal and professional life.

But I had a very big step left to take on this path. If the courage I needed depended on the meaningfulness of the challenges calling for it, then what I needed was the answer to one of life's oldest questions: *what makes things meaningful?*

I'll pass along a story that helped me answer this, a story, it's claimed, about the very first management consultant in history, sent by the pope to observe the construction of the cathedral of Notre Dame, in the twelfth century.

When the consultant arrived at the job site in Paris, he began talking to the workers. The first two were stonemasons, while the third was a little old lady whose job was to sweep up bits of broken stone.

The consultant asked the first mason what he was doing.

The man growled at him, "Can't you see, I'm a stonemason. I'm putting bread on my family's table."

The consultant asked the second mason the same question. This man waved his hand at the unfinished cathedral. "I'm working on a gargoyle that'll go on top of a buttress," he said.

The consultant then directed his question to the old woman. Now, it takes a century to build a cathedral, and this woman was going to be dead long before Notre Dame was finished. Nonetheless, she put down her broom and turned to look at where the grand spires would someday rise. Then she turned back to the consultant and said, "I, sir, am building a cathedral so people can talk to God."

The lesson from that old lady and from Lois Gibbs (and from my own life)—is that people who find real meaning in their lives don't find it in possessions or status. They find it in committing to ideals greater than themselves and their own needs, especially ideals of service. For Lois it was helping other people stay healthy. For the old woman it was helping people talk to God. In outdoor leadership, service might include keeping a team safe and on target, helping people through important personal hurdles, or finding other ways to enrich their lives.

Don't take my word for it. Look to your own experience. Isn't it this commitment to ideals bigger than yourself, especialy ideals of service, that creates the meaning in your life? And isn't it this commitment that generates the enthusiasm, passion, and power that you find in people who you perceive to be leading meaningful lives?

Now let's set this in the context of outdoor leadership. Recall Sally, the leader dealing with that nasty accident. Even though she's trained, experienced, and equipped to deal with her crisis, she's never before faced one this big. What will help pull her through now is focusing on the personal meaning she finds in the situation she's in.

What's meaningful about a bloody mess and a badly injured climber twelve miles from nowhere? The answer is the role that leadership plays in Sally's life. Sally has trained for years as a leader. With her expertise and experience, she has gained a quiet confidence that spills over into all the other parts of her life, affecting both her self-image and her relationships. She is also aware of and enjoys the positive effect her leadership has on other peoples' lives. Leading *means* something to her at a level that is profoundly personal, and this ties into the whole web of her values and priorities.

Sally knew from the beginning that sooner or later she'd have to deal with a situation that would push her to the limit; unconsciously, she may even have anticipated it. In any case, here it is. She's trained and ready— but what she has to do now will flow, not solely from her competence as a leader, but from her own deeply satisfying reasons for *why* she leads. If she's feeling jittery as she struggles to tend to the wounded climber, reminding herself of this will be a major source of the courage she now needs.

Consider a less happy situation. On another mountain trail, another leader, Chris, has to deal with a hiker doubled over with acute stomach pain. Chris is in a jam just as bad as Sally's. But while Chris is as technically competent as Sally, unlike her he has never felt comfortable in a leadership role. He leads climbs because it's expected of him; after all, he has been climbing for five years, and he has to do his part for the club.

All the knowledge, training, and experience in the world will not give Chris the courage in a crisis that a more profound sense of meaning for his leadership role might provide. But he can't focus on something that isn't there. Confronted with a rough situation, his first thought is not,

"I'm ready for this; let's go!" but "This shouldn't be happening to me!" He may still muddle through, but without the solid center that meaning provides, he will be more prone than Sally to panic, make bad decisions, and undermine the morale of his group.

One of the more bizarre adventures of my life provides a good illustration of the impact of meaning on courage.

In October 1980, I was on a cruise ship in the North Pacific that caught fire in the middle of the night. As the fire spread, 550 passengers and crew were directed into lifeboats. Because the ship was new, nobody expected it to catch fire, let alone sink; the lifeboat procedures were chaotic. Ninety-five people were wedged into our boat, which contained a big sign in the bow that read, "Capacity: 48."

This severe crowding ratcheted up the already high level of fear in that little boat. We were 140 miles from the Alaskan coast. Hypothermia was setting in, and an oncoming storm threatened to swamp us as we waited for dawn, the earliest that rescue helicopters could arrive.

There were a dozen members of the crew in that boat, including a couple of junior officers. None of them took charge. If anything, they whined and complained louder than anybody else. Suddenly, one of the crew stood up in that jam-packed, pitching vessel. Panicked out of his wits, he screamed that we were all going to die. Several other people started to weep. A wave of fear washed over the boat, drenching us like seawater.

All of a sudden, a woman in her seventies, a matron from one of New Jersey's oldest families, stood up next to the hysterical crewman and slapped him across the face. The man stopped yelling and stared at her, stunned, while she lectured him on his bad behavior. He sat down, shamefaced. The weeping stopped. Somebody started leading us in song. The moment of panic passed.

This magnificent lady was certainly no less aware of our dire circumstances than the crewmen. Nor do I think she was any less scared than the rest of us. Anyone who wasn't afraid in that lifeboat—feeling the hypothermia, watching the storm coming on—wasn't human.

What separated her from the crewmen was the meaning each saw in that desperate situation. Even with their training and professional responsibilities, the crewmen saw no deeper than saving their own skins. Professional pride and the safety of the group seemed to mean nothing to them.

But that matron had three hundred years of Yankee pride in her veins. Her people had always risen to the occasion, in body and in spirit.

Panic was unthinkable. Service to the public good was a given. Her courage seemed to flow automatically from how she viewed herself and her role in a situation of public need. When the helicopters finally arrived, she was the last woman to be rescued, and from the way she hesitated, I'm sure she would have preferred to have waited until all the men were safe as well.

■

The only way to get stronger in the face of fear is to move through that fear. If, as a leader, you're in a position to help someone move through fear, you're helping them through a crucial step in their lives. Fear is the Number One debilitating emotion. Fear of anything—of heights, of dying, of failure—is what will hold you back. You've got to admit it, deal with it, and transcend it.

In my very first mountaineering experience, I shattered my ankle—and as soon as I was healed, I went right back up that same mountain. I got trampled by a horse—so I learned to ride. I almost drowned—then I took up scuba diving.

Courageous people don't get involved in risky activities because it's "cool" or the "in" thing to do, or because somebody else told them to do it. They get involved because those activities mean a lot to them at a personal level. Once they're clear on that, then they take total responsibility for being in that risky situation, and are better able to deal with it.

Everyone goes through fear. The ones who survive are the ones who face it, and move on. If you don't, then you can become stuck, dissatisfied—even angry. You have to push through the discomfort, staying focused on your goal.

—Laura Evans, President/CEO,
Expeditions Inspiration and author of *The Climb of My Life*

■

The importance of being a role model. There's one final lesson from my hero from New Jersey—about the power of role models in crisis situations. When the man in the lifeboat panicked, some of the tourists aboard started to follow his lead, since they figured he was a member of the crew and therefore must know. What the matron did was to present a far more powerful alternative model, which is what it took to shift the mood and behavior of the group.

Especially in the outdoors, times may come when accidents, weather, or fate will severely test you and your group. If someone in your group starts to panic, your example as leader is crucial. Remind yourself of the factors that will increase your control in those situations. Focus on the core meaning you ascribe to being a leader. Then act with the courage you need—to meet the challenge, and to inspire others to follow your lead.

A leader needs to be cocky and confident—and borderline paranoid—all at the same time.

You have to be an optimist to be courageous, to be able to deal with situations that are out of hand, or that could get out of hand. Your optimism is key, because leaders are role models, one way or the other. The leader's attitude is crucial to your group. Leaders can't come unglued.

—Peter Whittaker, climber/guide, Summits Adventure Travel

Courage can be a surprising feature in people. I've seen people who've trained for years but who fell apart in a crisis. I've seen others who seemed least competent but who performed very well.

The people who I see performing best in a crisis are people who are honest and forthright. They don't hide their personalities or their weaknesses. They're genuine. What this tells me is that these people have ego strength. The people who feel they have to protect their egos are the ones most likely to come apart in a crisis.

I once worked with a guy leading heli-ski trips. This guy had all the skills, but was no good when things got tough. He was more concerned with protecting his image than getting the job done. One afternoon, for example, he was in the lead and I could see he was heading down a bad slope. I called for him to stop but he wouldn't. Sure enough, we all had to climb back up. From that point on, his decision making got really weird and dangerous, because he felt he'd lost face. For this man, I think his self-image was the only thing keeping him together.

Courage in an outdoors leader is also about being able to say no. I've guided heli-ski trips where we've been dropped on top of beautiful, untouched, 30-degree slopes. Unfortunately, I can see and sense that these perfect slopes are severe avalanche risks, so I turn my group in another direction. When I do, some client angrily says, "Are you nuts?" and complains that he's not getting his money's worth.

Whether it's heli-skiing or whatever, in cases like this, you've simply got to stand your ground: you explain the reasons for your decision, and, in my case, I reconfirm my intention of finding great skiing and keeping everybody alive. But you don't back down. If you do cave, your group will walk all over you from then on, and your credibility is shot.

—Sharon Wood, Adventure Dynamics,
first North American woman to summit on Everest

Courage

❑ **What is courage?** Courage is facing what scares you, including risks that test your spirit as well as your body. Courage is the ability to do the right thing, and do it well, even when you're afraid.

❑ **The amount of courage you need to cope with a situation is proportional to the risks you perceive.** This suggests two basic strategies: you can reduce the perceived risks and/or summon up the courage necessary to deal with them.

❑ **Reduce perceived risks by increasing control.** You can do this by:
   ▪ increasing your knowledge;
   ▪ acquiring the right tools;
   ▪ gaining experience; and
   ▪ getting help.

   ▪ *Dealing with panic.* If someone in your group starts to lose control:
      ▪ make clear your genuine concern for the other;
      ▪ speak clearly, calmly, and honestly about the situation and your strategy for improving it;
      ▪ describe in detail the next steps to be taken;
      ▪ if there's time, tell stories about times when you were scared;
      ▪ maintain your sense of humor.

   ▪ *Preparing for next time.* No matter how well you handled the last crisis, look for ways to increase the factors that will help you feel even more in control next time around.

❑ **Find courage by finding meaning.** People who are good at taking risks focus on the meaning that risky situations have for them. They embark on risky activities knowing that what they are doing makes sense to them at the deepest level of their being.

❑ **The importance of being a role model.** Especially if someone in your group starts to panic, your example as leader is crucial.

Chapter Eleven

Team Building: Visionary Leadership

Team building is a complex and comprehensive process, which requires clear thinking, common sense, and a caring heart. But its most important element is your ability to create and communicate a vision of results that inspires action, moves individuals to perform at their best, and helps create the cohesion, guidance, and momentum needed for success.

Every task that requires complex, coordinated effort requires teamwork, whether you're rowing an eight-oared shell, climbing an 8,000-meter peak, or organizing a beach clean-up.

A good team is far more than a group of people committed to a common goal. A good team is a magical enterprise, because it can make the total effort of its members more than the sum of what each of them could do alone.

I rowed crew in college, and I loved it. Part of my enthusiasm stemmed from knowing that rowing kept me in such great shape for climbing. But I loved rowing for an even more powerful reason: the synergy the sport both created and demanded. For the first time in my life, I was part of a team, in a sport in which, if you're any good at all, teamwork is both exquisite and complete. When the eight of us in that boat were swinging back and forth in perfect rhythm and balance, we could all feel the added power created not by any one of us, but by the whole. We became one spirit, one pulling machine—one team.

———————————

Team building is essential for efforts that are large, long, and complex. But the process is also useful for smaller initiatives as well. You won't need a perfectly coordinated team for a weekend snowshoe trip, but any team building you do will be a plus, especially if there's conflict or crisis in those few days.

Building and leading teams draw on all the qualities of good leadership, including planning, making good decisions, taking responsibility, caring, communicating, and dealing with conflict and stress. Here, it all comes together. This chapter will take you from the initial step of forming your team, to building trust among team members, to forming a vision that can inspire and guide your team to reach its goals.

Choose team members with care. The "magic" that can make the team more than the sum of its parts needs decent raw material. Are all your people qualified and equipped for this enterprise? Does your team collectively have the necessary strengths and skills to reach its goals? If not, can you recruit people who are capable of filling the gaps?

In some cases, such as club trips, your power to hand-pick your team may be limited. Still, at least you have veto power. Be ready to use it. While no one likes to say no, you have too much at stake to allow people along on your trip who are not qualified.

Reach early agreement on your team's goals. If you don't have enough clarity about goals, you're asking for trouble. If half your team is determined to bag the peak even if it takes a bivouac in the rain while the other half thinks it signed up for a fair-weather climb, you're going to have a problem if the weather breaks. Discuss and confirm agreement on team goals early in the planning stage. Then talk about contingency plans. Gain at least general agreement on what the team will do in case its original goals are not reachable.

Early discussion of, and agreement on, goals and contingency plans is good insurance. It's similar to the co-pilot announcing your destination before closing the main cabin door. I've yet to see some red-faced soul bolt for the exit, but someday—you never know.

■

Part of the responsibility of being a leader is to establish and keep to ground rules. People need to know from the beginning what they can and can't do.

> The leader also must make sure that everybody knows that success (in reaching a summit, for example) is not a given. The first thing I say to a new group of people whom I'm about to lead out on a trip that could be dangerous is: "I hope everybody has something important to do after this trip." Then I explain that I want them to know that this is not a trip in which we go for the summit at all costs. I say we have a great chance to get to the summit, but we may also have to turn back, and I want all their support if we have to do that.
> —Peter Whittaker, climber/guide, Summits Adventure Travel
>
> ■

Honor differences. People have widely differing skills, personalities, quirks, and gifts. David and Ann are excellent backcountry skiers but often forget to slow down for others; Jason, though he's out of shape, could navigate out of a whiteout in Antarctica; Ian's not the best skier, but his sense of humor is a big plus; and Jennifer's analytical mind drives some people nuts but is a real asset in planning.

Your job as leader is to find the best possible ways these attributes can complement each other. Start by acknowledging each person's strengths. This will make everyone feel needed, as well as let the more compulsive members relax, knowing that they don't have to know or do everything.

On a good team, contrary opinions become assets rather than liabilities. Good teams are never made up of robots, nor are goals and priorities ever pronounced from on high. Rather, they are syntheses, the products of contributions, discussions, and yes, even arguments, among people who trust each other enough that when they do disagree, each person's effort is not to promote one point of view at all costs, but to look for common ground.

Delegate authority. One benefit of delegating authority is that you don't have to do all the work yourself. Another benefit is that it builds teamwork. When people feel they are integral parts of the action, their commitment to the enterprise, and to the team, grows. As it grows, so does their willingness to take more responsibility for achieving team goals.

Delegating authority can be tricky, however, and should only be done after you've assessed the strengths and preferences of individual team members. Try to fit the right people to the right tasks. If the matches leave too much to be desired, don't delegate.

■

> I work in emergency search and rescue (SAR) operations in one of the busiest national parks in Canada. We're responsible for anyone who comes into the park and gets into trouble—mountaineers, hikers, skiers.
> I'm a firm believer in teamwork. I depend on it, especially in

avalanche search and rescues in which the pressure is intense and an immediate response is essential. If a person is buried in an avalanche, the clock starts ticking, and if an hour, or sometimes even thirty minutes, goes by, that person is going to be dead.

There's a lot going on all at once in an avalanche rescue, and it's difficult to keep everything straight in your head. Everything comes down on you at once. So the leader is very dependent on the skills and resources of others.

I know leaders who say, "I'm the leader, and I know all the answers." I say, "I know I'm human." I know I need others to check on me, and to make suggestions. I know I can dash out the door and forget my gloves.

We use a team technique we call "shadowing" on our avalanche search and rescues: in addition to the designated leader, we also assign a "shadow leader"—usually a person of similar skills and ability to the designated leader on site. This shadow leader doesn't participate actively in the rescue but stands 20 yards away on the edge of the avalanche scene. He takes a detached view, observing and assessing results. He can often see key things that the designated leader is missing and can suggest improvements.

—Tim Auger, Public Safety Specialist,
Search and Rescue, Banff National Park

■

Create a team bond through building trust. Bonding gives a team the capacity to move as a whole. Individual needs and priorities are not forgotten but are subsumed to those of the team. This isn't experienced as a sacrifice, because each team member perceives the bond as beneficial. Bonding doesn't always occur, but when it does, the whole becomes more than the sum of its parts.

Alignment around a common goal may help bond a team but may also produce mere marriages of convenience that dissipate quickly as soon as the goal is met or abandoned. Stable bonding, which goes much deeper, occurs when team members learn to trust each other.

Trust has several facets. Technical competence helps build trust within a team. For example, if everyone with you on a backcountry ski trip is an expert in avalanche rescue techniques, you're going to trust them more with your safety than if they were rank beginners. Accountability—knowing that everyone with you will fulfill his or her role—helps build trust, too.

But the crucial factor in building trust within a team is caring for the people you're with. Caring starts with you. When your team members feel that you as leader appreciate their needs and interests, their trust that you will consistently act for the good of the group grows. And as you model the ability to put yourself in others' shoes, they will pick up on your example. In this way, the caring you show as leader starts to build trust among the entire team.

Technical competence, accountability, and caring build trust. Trust builds bonds. And all of this trust building takes both time and shared experience. The results are worth it.

Three weeks into the Harvard climb up the north wall of Mount McKinley, our team had crossed all the dangerous avalanche chutes at the bottom of the face and scaled the tricky rock wall that led to the easier ice pitches above. A good part of our success was due to the fact that we'd been climbing together for over a year. We joked that we knew each other better than our mothers did—and that wasn't much of an exaggeration. Now, having come through a difficult and dangerous piece of climbing together, we figured we had it made.

After a hard night of hauling up gear from lower camps, we pitched our tents on a flat expanse of hard snow, protected on the uphill side by a 15-foot ice cliff. Late that afternoon, we awoke to start the next night's climb. Rick crawled out of his tent first, then ambled a few feet ahead and began to pee a hole in the snow. Suddenly that hole grew bigger and bigger as the yellow snow began to fall away into a crevasse so deep, he could not see the bottom. We had pitched the entire camp on a fragile snow bridge over a monster void.

Rick stared, then carefully backtracked to the tents and quietly told us that we were, at that moment, pulling on our socks on top of at least 200 feet of air. "Yeah, right," said Don, throwing a smelly sock at him. Chris, older and perhaps wiser, crawled out to check the report. "Hey guys, he's not kidding," he said a few seconds later, his voice slightly unsteady.

One at a time we slowly and carefully got out of the tents, pulled the stakes, and then gently dragged or carried everything out of harm's way. Each of the seven of us did exactly what he needed to do, choreographing our moves to put the least possible strain on the snow bridge that supported us. I don't remember a word being said. All this probably took five minutes, but it seemed forever.

I know now it was the bond we'd formed as a team that let us move so quickly and efficiently, virtually as one. There were plenty of times when we didn't agree on that trip, but never a time when we couldn't realign. Some of the trust that cemented that bond came from knowing that each one of us was competent at his job. But even more of that glue came from knowing and caring for one another.

That level of bonding is not the norm. A far more likely situation would be starting a trip with a bunch of people who don't know each other, and for whom trust building has to start virtually from scratch. Start by having people introduce themselves, perhaps using some goofy game to help break the ice. Use break times for informal conversations with people you don't know, and encourage others to do the same. Try to put yourself in others' boots, especially if you see them running into difficulties. Draw from some of the approaches suggested in Chapter Seven. And be patient: building trust takes time.

Recognize potential problems early. People don't always perform as you'd wish. Bonds don't always form. Be on the lookout for the kinds of little frictions and mistakes that might grow into big trouble later on. Maintain a 360-degree view. Is any team member more lacking in needed skills than you thought? Are those snide remarks between Ann and Jerry going to build into a nasty fight just when you need people to pull together? Could Simon's gung-ho attitude lead him to underestimate risks?

If you're on the alert for signs such as these, you'll be able to take remedial actions to minimize the chances for real problems later on. For example, you can reassign responsibilities among team members, mediate disputes before they get out of hand, and quietly express your concerns to any team members whose actions worry you. Interventions such as these may not completely solve the problems, but by addressing them early and openly, you'll at least have the chance to diminish them and/or compensate for their effects.

■

A big part of a leader's responsibility is knowing who's on the team, and planning accordingly. I do a lot of team workshops with corporations, and one bunch of company execs I was with insisted that they wanted to go river rafting. Since our service was oriented toward climbing, we contracted with some river guides to take these clients rafting down a fairly difficult river. One of the rafts turned over and got pinned against some rocks. Everybody got out and nobody got hurt, at least initially.

But these clients were all very "can-do," people, and some of them decided that they had to "help" free the pinned raft. They all started clambering over wet rocks trying to fix a situation in which they had no expertise. The river guides could not or would not exercise any control, and the chaos built. One guy ended up breaking his ankle. The river guides completely lost credibility because of their failure to lead.

In my opinion, their mistakes started earlier than that. They failed to assess who they were leading. They should have known that a gung-ho bunch of superachieving executives would insist on taking charge in an emergency. They should have known how to divert that energy into useful support. Instead, what was a minor mishap turned into a fairly major thing.

—Sharon Wood, Adventure Dynamics,
first North American woman to summit on Everest

■

Create and communicate a vision of success. A crucial factor in building and leading teams is creating a vision, a clear, concrete picture of intended results that is shared by the entire team. If it's powerful enough, a vision can chart the course, inspire the commitment, and create the momentum needed to make that picture a reality. Creating and communicating a vision will improve the odds for success in any complex and difficult project, whether in the outdoors or not. Almost all major political movements, for example, have started with just such powerful visions.

Martin Luther King had no reason to be optimistic that day, nor did the thousands of people waiting impatiently for him to begin speaking. The civil rights movement had fierce opponents. There was no money. The people looking up at King knew these things, and many of them were discouraged. They looked at the solitary figure behind the rostrum and they waited for leadership—and hope.

King talked briefly about some of the specific challenges facing the movement, and then shifted to what he really had come to say. "I have a dream," he said, and began to create a vision of a country that could be but was not yet. King's dream became both a source of inspiration and a blueprint for political action.

Visions such as Dr. King's aren't fantasies; they aren't hopes or wishes. Visions are detailed pictures of the expected results of the creativity, energy, and spirit of the person or persons involved. Visions are pictures of what will be, but is not yet.

Visions and team building. Visions are effective in helping individuals reach personal goals, whether those might be finding the perfect mate, getting through law school, or climbing every 8,000-meter peak in the world. Athletes have been using visions for decades to improve their performance. Studies show, for example, that basketball players who spend time off court "seeing" their shots go through the hoop improve their shooting percentages almost as much as players who actually practice with the ball.

The most dramatic power of visions, however, is not in improving individual performance but in building and leading teams—in catalyzing, guiding, coordinating, and encouraging groups of people to take on difficult and complex challenges.

- Visions can inspire action, often at an extraordinary level.
- Visions can help create and maintain momentum, that hard-to-define shift in mood that lends extra power, focus, and determination to a team exactly when needed.
- Visions can keep organizations and teams focused on end results. A powerful vision is often the "glue" that keeps team members working together effectively, despite stresses and distractions.
- Visions can be powerful tools for resolving conflicts and planning complex projects, issues covered in Chapter Fifteen.

Creating a vision. The kinds of outdoors challenges that benefit from visionary leadership include everything from leading an expedition to the Himalayas to coping with an unexpected emergency on a family outing.

It's mid-October and Leona, Ted, and their two children are on a long-delayed backpacking trip deep into a wilderness area that has been a favorite of theirs for years. Winter usually comes late to this area, and the radio reports had promised four days of decent weather—but the reports were wrong. On the second night, a fierce, unseasonable storm catches the family 6 miles from the trailhead, 8 from the ranger station at Cache Creek. The temperature drops into the teens, the winds rise to gale force, and over a foot of snow falls before dawn.

The family stays in its tent all the next day, waiting out the storm. Ted and Leona play word games with fifteen-year-old Paula and twelve-year-old Kevin. Both kids are old enough to recognize the danger the family is in, and they're scared.

By the second night, the snowfall has abated, but the winds have not. The temperature has dropped close to zero. Two of the tent seams are stretching dangerously. Kevin's lightweight sleeping bag is useless, and only climbing in with his father keeps him from hypothermia.

At first light, the weather is no better, but Leona and Ted decide they have to make a break for it. The tent will shred very soon, and even staying inside, all of them are dangerously cold. They have no snowshoes. Their car is undoubtedly snowed in, which means they have to make it to the ranger station. It's going to take an extraordinary effort to get them all down safely.

Kneeling in the tent, Ted shows everyone the compass and contour maps, and points out the route down: they'll stay just high enough on the ridge to avoid heavy drifts. To keep everyone together, Leona ties each person in with a short length of heavy cord she found in her pack. They all put on every piece of warm clothing they've got.

These practical elements are essential, but they're not going to be enough—not if somebody panics and gets hurt, not if someone loses hope and sits down in the snow. The family is badly in need of something that will lift their spirits, calm their fears, and focus their minds on what they need to do to get through the crisis.

That "something" is a vision. What Leona and Ted must do now is create and communicate a vision of success that everyone in the family can share. Each of them needs to "see" a safe descent in detail.

Leona begins. "I can already picture us getting out of here. It's dinnertime tonight. We're all in the Hungry Bear Cafe and Motel, across the road from the ranger station, warming ourselves in front of the fire, waiting for our food to come. The motel only had one room left, but it sure beats the tent!"

Ted, closing his eyes for a moment, adds to the vision. "I've just ordered the biggest steak in the house, and the smells from the grill are drifting under our noses. Any minute now the waitress is going to come out with a big tray heaped with food. Meanwhile we're all telling stories of how we got down off this mountain. I'm remembering how good it felt to reach the road, knowing that the ranger station and Hungry Bear were just down the hill."

He opens his eyes. "Now who else is with me at the Hungry Bear; who's got a story?"

At first, Paula looks at her parents as if they have lost their senses. "You guys," she says, her voice breaking slightly, "how can you play games when we're all about to get blown off this mountain? Don't you know how serious this is?"

Ted looks at his daughter, then says calmly, "Your mother and I know what our situation is. But I don't think we're quite ready to crawl out that tent door yet. Trust us—what we're doing will help get us ready—and it'll only take a few minutes. Will you help?"

"What the heck," Paula says. "I guess I'll play. I'm in the cafe, too. I'm looking at the snow still melting off my parka, hanging by the fire, and I'm thinking how happy I am that it kept me dry all the way down, especially when piles of snow kept falling on us from the trees. My hair's still wet from the best hot shower I ever had. Boy, was I lucky that Kevin left any hot water at all!"

"Yeah, right," says Kevin. "Notice it wasn't *me* we had to wait for at the motel. Anyway, I've got my feet up near the fireplace, looking at Paula's parka, too. I'm glad it's yellow 'cause I could see it even through the fog and snow. And I'm glad Mom made me put that waterproofing gunk on my boots—it really worked, even when we were kicking through those huge drifts. I was afraid we couldn't get through snow that deep, but I followed the leader, like Dad always says to do, and it wasn't so bad. But I sure am ready for my burger!"

"Hey, give a little credit to the navigators," says Leona. "I took bearings every 50 feet, even in the storm, and your dad and I stuck to the right contour of the ridge even at that tricky part near the bottom."

Element by element, the pictures of success for the family become clearer and more complete, until they've all but choreographed the entire trip down. As they continue to visualize a successful journey, they allow their emotions to accompany the pictures, making it all the more real. Their vision strengthens, and they become more focused on what they need to do. When images of the descent and the happy gathering at the Hungry Bear Cafe are vivid for all of them, they are ready for the real trip down.

■

Teams work when there's a shared vision and, from that, shared objectives, strategy, philosophy, and style. On the 1986 Everest West Ridge Expedition, we started, in many ways, as a very mixed bag of thirteen individuals. But each of us was chosen because we had a record of being a good team player. Once we had a core of five, it took a consensus of all team members to add each of the next eight.

The expedition leader asked each one of us three questions: Why are you here? What strengths do you bring? What could you get out of this, whether or not you get to the top? Initially these questions seemed strange. But asking and answering questions such as these built a strong common thread, a strong philosophical base. It showed respect for all members. It recognized everybody's strengths. I felt like a valuable, contributing member of the group from then on.

—Sharon Wood, Adventure Dynamics,
first North American woman to summit on Everest

■

Essential qualities of a vision. Not every picture in your mind is a vision. There are certain attributes a vision must have to succeed. A vision needs to:

- be clear and concrete—so sharp and detailed that you can see, smell, and taste it. Huddled in that tent, Kevin must be able to taste that hamburger in order to make credible his vision of being in the cafe. He has to feel his boots crunching into the trail broken by the rest of his family for the vision of a careful, safe descent to be real to him. Although still in that tent, everyone in the family needs to see themselves staying on their route despite the storm. They need to experience a rush of relief at reaching the road, and feel the warmth of the fire at the cafe.
- be positive. Don't try to motivate yourself or others with a vision of the bad things that might happen if you don't succeed. A vision based on fear may fuel immediate action, but it will also cripple creative and courageous thinking, and may cause panic. Ted and Leona don't try to motivate their team by creating a picture of all of them freezing to death if they fail. They know that a vision based on hope, not fear, is a far better motivator.
- include a clear picture of the power and impact of your own role. Your overall purpose is to inspire and motivate your team. But in working to create a vision, don't forget to put yourself in the picture so that you'll be motivated, too. Ted and Leona need to fully share the vision they are creating for their family.
- be open to the contributions of others. The leader's role as initiator of a visioning process is key. But visions motivate best when team members feel they've also had a role in creating them. That's why Ted and Leona patiently coax their kids to join in. In doing so, they not only end up with a stronger vision, but every member of the family accepts the vision as his or her own.

  Take the time to invite team members to contribute to the vision of team success. You'll probably find some initial reluctance; if strong, then don't use the word *vision* at all. Ask the team to join you in creating pictures of what they want to have happen. Spell out the benefits you expect.

  Many people will overcome their hesitations once they hear you begin. Sharing your vision gives others permission to follow your lead. And once engaged, they'll start to feel the same excitement you do, and the process will take off. Think of it as an impromptu dip in a mountain lake on a hot August hike. Everybody stares at the water—until one person jumps in.
- come from the heart. Don't try to think your way to a vision. Applying brain power is vital at the other points in the process. But to create a vision, you have to give way to the nonrational part of yourself, and give yourself the freedom to see and feel what doesn't yet exist.

I am a great believer in vision leadership. Climbing is a wonderful metaphor for vision leadership because a mountain is *something you can see.* You see a crystalline peak piercing the blue sky, and a great desire to *be there* comes over you. The picture of yourself atop that lofty mountain embeds itself in your mind. From then until you attain your goal, a certain spiritual discomfort settles into your soul that will only be vanquished when you either attain the summit or give up your dream.

Of course, your dream may not be a summit. It may be a new route on a rock wall, or climbing an established route a new way. Whatever the goal, once you have the picture, the key is to hold it, and not give up. Failure comes from giving up.

In my career as a climber, the most dramatic example of this truth occurred during my solo ascent of the John Muir Route on El Capitan. My predecessors, Yvon Chouinard and TM Herbert, had put up a magnificent route. I was pushed to my limit. Seven days out I was still 1,000 feet from the top. I was wrung out. I was useless. I was *used up.* Going down began to look very attractive. I began the process of convincing myself the situation was hopeless. But the vision of successfully climbing it alone had taken such a firm grip on my mind that the picture fought back against the developing image of surrender. As my mind wavered between my vision of success and giving up, I held on just long enough to the positive picture to allow a kind of answer to come through: I would just do the next 5 feet. And the next. And the next. It seems you can always do 5 more feet. I kept that up until I got to the top. Holding to the vision got me there.

In 1991, when my company got into serious trouble, and we were looking at the real possibility of failure, I used the vision principle to pull us out. I had a vision of survival. The thing I had to do that I had never consciously had to do before was to *build a shared vision* with the rest of my team. Once everyone had a clear picture of survival as our central mission, my job became *chief encourager.* I had to keep the picture vivid and alive and real. As long as the picture of survival was burning in the mind of every team member, we would move toward that vision, and anything less than reaching it was simply not in our reality screen. Driven by the vision, we found new and better ways to do things, new and better ways to work together, new and better ways to serve the customer. People more than ever parked their egos at the door and devoted themselves to the good of the company. Our improvement began to look like the picture in our minds. We returned to health and vigorous growth. Holding to the shared vision was the key.

—Royal Robbins, President, Royal Robbins Company

Anyone can create and communicate a vision. Creating a vision requires that you be willing to shut down your mind temporarily, and let your spirit lead. You can't create a vision by thinking about it. You have to feel your way there, suspending your disbelief about pictures changing the world.

If you're the kind of person who's been relentlessly logical from birth, using visions as serious tools for leadership may be a new challenge. If so, practice on yourself before trying to use visions with others. Start with something small, for which failure is no catastrophe. Using the guidance in this chapter, create a vision of results for a minor goal at work, or in your family, and use it as a guide and motivator. As you see the benefits, you'll gain confidence about using visions with larger, more important projects, and about communicating them to others. Whatever the task, learning to create and communicate visions will consistently raise the odds for getting the results you want.

Those results may be in building and leading teams, or in dealing with difficult people and handling conflicts—subjects covered in the next chapter.

Team Building: Visionary Leadership

❑ **A good team coordinates the contributions of its members** so that their total effort will be more than the sum of what each of them could do alone.

❑ **Choose team members with care.**

❑ **Reach early agreement on your team's goals**—and contingency plans if those goals prove out of reach.

❑ **Honor differences.** Find the best possible ways the different attributes of team members can complement each other. On a good team, contrary opinions become assets rather than liabilities.

❑ **Delegate authority.** When people feel they are integral parts of the action, their commitment to the enterprise, and to the team, grows.

❑ **Create a team bond through building trust.** The most important factor in building trust is caring for the people you're with.

❑ **Recognize potential problems early** so you can take remedial action to minimize the chances for real problems later on.

❑ **Create and communicate a vision of success**—a clear, concrete picture of intended results.

   ■ *Visions and team building.* The most dramatic power of visions is in building and leading teams—in catalyzing, guiding, coordinating, and encouraging groups of people to take on difficult and complex challenges.

   ■ *Creating a vision: essential qualities.* To succeed, a vision must:
      ■ be clear and concrete;
      ■ be positive;
      ■ include a clear picture of the power and impact of your own role;
      ■ be open to the contributions of others; and
      ■ come from the heart.

   ■ *Anyone can create and communicate a vision.* Start with something small, then move to larger and more important projects as you gain confidence.

Chapter Twelve

Resolving Conflicts

The real issues driving any conflict are rarely the obvious ones—you must dig deeper for the answers. Center your strategy for resolving conflicts around building trust. Aim not for compromise but for innovative solutions built on genuinely common ground.

Conflicts in outdoors situations are inevitable. The challenge is to head them off when you can—and deal with them effectively when you can't.

You're leading a rafting trip down a section of the Roughwater River that you know can get very dangerous this time of year. Two others in your group are expert rafters, but everybody else is a beginner. It's been raining hard up in the mountains for two days and the river is high. That's not a problem for the first leg of the trip, but now your group has made it to Devil's Fork, where the river splits in two. The right-hand channel is no more difficult than what you've already experienced. But the left channel has serious rapids, even without the recent rains. You don't have a firsthand report of conditions, but you assume the left fork is too dangerous for the group you're leading.

When you tell the group that you're thinking of heading down the right fork, everybody nods—except Dan and Nora, who are at least as experienced as you as white-water rafters and challenge your assessment as being too conservative. They describe the trip down the left fork as "the adventure of a lifetime," and start recruiting two more people to make a full raftload. Several beginners are being swayed by their challenge.

You're tempted by their arguments—it *would* be a great ride. But you also know it would be irresponsible to take that degree of risk with this group. You tell everyone the decision's made—it's the right fork. With the water this high, you say, the only way any raft should go down the left fork is with a crew of four expert paddlers.

Privately, you also know that even if two people with the experience of Dan and Nora could make it down on their own, that would leave you alone with two overloaded rafts of beginners—not a safe situation even on the "easy" fork. You tell Dan and Nora that the whole group has to stick together, and that it will take the easier fork.

A discussion turns into an argument turns into a shouting match. Suddenly you have something like a mutiny on your hands. What do you do?

This situation isn't so hypothetical, as anyone who's been leading in the outdoors for a while can attest.

The strategy that follows comes out of my experiences in dealing with conflicts of many kinds, from disputes on outdoor trips to wrestling with Russians and Cubans while in the Foreign Service to environmental battles in the Pacific Northwest.

It's a strategy that depends for its success not on outwitting or overpowering your opponent, but on creating the trust needed to find and build on common ground, and on creating a vision of results that benefits all sides. These elements of trust building, common ground, and vision make this strategy not only unusual, but unusually effective.

The strategy applies to any conflict, not only to those you may encounter in outdoor leadership. People are people, and when things start getting out of hand, their emotional responses and interpersonal dynamics are about the same no matter what the fight is about or where it occurs.

■

It's crazy some of the fights people get into. I heard about two climbers once—smart guys with Ph.D.s—who got into a fight on a glacier in South America because they couldn't agree how to divide up a can of sardines. They ended up trying to kill each other with their ice axes. Sure, sometimes you can say, oh, it's the altitude, or it's fatigue. But there's no excuse for fighting. Prevent conflict before it starts. Compliment people, even if they might not deserve it. Be friendly. Be willing to compromise when you have to. Don't make bad guys out of anybody.
—Paul Petzoldt, founder of the National Outdoor Leadership School

■

Dealing with conflict often becomes free-form in style. You may find that some of the steps in this strategy don't apply to your situation, or you may need to apply them in some creative new combination of your own.

Start by readying your own heart and mind, then explore the many avenues for building trust. Building trust can lead to common ground; common ground can lead to a shared vision of success; and that shared vision can translate to real solutions that work for all sides.

Remember: *you* **are in charge of how you respond, no matter what the provocation.** Dealing with emotions is almost always harder than dealing with the issues that spark them. An out-of-control reaction from you means the provoker is in control. Out there on the Roughwater River, it serves no good purpose to blame Dan and Nora for goading you into losing your cool, no matter how rude their manners or nasty their language.

You're trying to read a book and the kids are making a racket in the next room; it's raining so they can't go outside. You can scream at them that you've had a hard week and they'd better shut up; figure that their loud play is unavoidable, remember what a rainy day was like when you were a kid, and go back to your book; or forget the book and join the kids in a Monopoly game—after all, you've hardly seen them all week. The provocation is exactly the same in all three cases—it's what you do with it that's different.

Be aware of preformed judgments you may have of people who see the issue differently, and/or act in ways you don't like. It's true that Dan often seems grouchy and combative, and that Nora has that annoying air of superiority about her. But if your first move in dealing with the situation is to hang those judgments on them, you'll be creating self-fulfilling prophecies and undermining your chances of success. By at least initially giving Dan and Nora the benefit of the doubt, you risk little while giving them room to rise to their best.

And don't forget, from their point of view, Dan and Nora may only be reacting to negative judgments they have of *you*. By giving them the benefit of the doubt, you challenge their negative judgments and provide an incentive for them to reexamine their own tired assessments.

Be especially careful to avoid damaging judgments of slower or less proficient members of any group you lead. Ken may well need to get himself in better physical shape, or get more training, and perhaps you'll have a private opportunity to kindly suggest that. But when he finally does straggle to the top of the ridge, greet him with an enthusiastic hello instead of a look of long-suffering patience or ill-concealed disdain. Moral judgments, whether made with words or body language, will probably make Ken less likely to go to the gym or take a training course. He'll judge *you* as imperious and rude, and that will let him take the pressure off himself to improve.

■

It pays to give difficult people the benefit of the doubt. On the Everest West Ridge Expedition in 1986, we'd just been blown off the mountain and had started back up for one last try. We were down to a team of two climbers who had enough strength left to make a try for the summit. Three other climbers, however, had volunteered to support getting us in position to make the summit attempt.

On the first day of this last trip back up, we covered only two-thirds of the distance we had intended, because of bad conditions. Huddled together in a protected spot, we had all but decided to give up. Then one of the support climbers came up, and I saw it was someone who I really didn't like; we just didn't get along at all and had spent a good part of the expedition avoiding each other. Now here he comes, and he sees us ready to turn back. "Heck," he says, "I'm not going to give up! I didn't spend the last four years preparing for this to turn around now. I'm going on!"

The rest of us took a look at each other—and followed him up. What I initially took to be this man's sheer stubbornness motivated all of us. But it was more than that. We'd all been focused on the immediate pain and fatigue, and he pushed us to see a bigger picture. If this guy had also given up, I'm sure we all would have gone back down. He knew he personally didn't have the gas to go on to the summit, but he pushed the rest of us to go on, on the strength of the vision of success we all shared. I finally saw that what was driving him was not stubbornness alone, but his total commitment and his integrity—and this changed my picture of him considerably.

—Sharon Wood, Adventure Dynamics,
first North American woman to summit on Everest

■

Understand that the real issues driving any conflict are rarely the obvious ones. Any conflict is like an iceberg with seven-eighths of its mass below the water line. Hidden there may be residues of slights and failures and disappointments from last week. But it's the deeper stuff that creates the real problems. Buried at the bottom of the iceberg may be issues of authority and control that date back to childhood and are surrounded by powerful feelings. People whose behavior seems consistently angry, insulting, bullying, or hostile, for example, often suffer from an underlying lack of self-confidence which has been feeding on them since they were kids.

No one's asking you to play psychotherapist on the trail. But it would be naive to ignore the way buried issues—and the surrounding emotions— can make people defensive, unreasonable, and combative. The more aware you are of these buried issues, the better able you'll be to deal with the conflict.

■

As a leader, I have had to deal with homophobic, racist, and ageist group members. As a coworker, I have seen religious feuds and abortion disputes break out in the middle of the woods (one even came to physical blows). In most cases, the intolerant behavior of one or two individuals threatened the authority of the leader and/or the integrity of the group.

People resent and judge leaders and group members for any number of reasons: fear and anger seem to be the keys—they exist for everyone to some degree. It is critical that leaders learn to recognize intolerant behavior (within the group and within themselves), and understand its destructive potential. The leader must set and defend a tone of tolerance. Differences must be respected so that the group remains unified toward the larger common goal. If bigoted behavior is allowed to express itself, the group and/or leader is threatened.

Suzanne Hanlon, Tours Director, Adventure Cycling Association

■

The key to success in dealing with conflict is to build trust between you and your opponent(s). Trust? When some ignorant jerk is yelling in my face? There's a choice to be made here. You can deal with conflict the way most people do: you can react to negative behavior by launching some of your own, and then watch the situation spiral out of control. Or you can try building trust. I've kept score on this one for many years, and I guarantee that a strategy based on building trust will consistently bring you better results in dealing with conflict than one based on spitting in your opponent's eye.

I'm not talking about building the degree of trust you might need to ask someone to donate a kidney or be godfather to your only child. I'm talking about developing the kind of trust that allows you to say, "OK, we disagree. But I think you're being honest. I think you really want to do the right thing. And I see that you listen. I'm willing to respond in kind."

One immediate effect you'll notice from a strategy of building trust is its shock value. Building trust breaks the rules of the tired old game of blame and counterblame, and can reverse the negative momentum of a conflict that has begun to move in vicious circles.

As trust develops, communication becomes easier, more honest, and less defensive; even difficult people begin to feel safe enough to open up in ways they wouldn't have risked before. Everyone calms down enough to allow options to appear that couldn't be seen or heard before in the heat of battle.

If you sense there are difficult people along, go out of your way early to open dialogue and take actions that build trust. You can't change deep-seated negative behaviors in a day, but you can defuse those behaviors, and make them less likely to erupt into full-scale conflict. Difficult people find it harder to justify their bad behavior, even to themselves, if they can't blame someone else for whatever they think is going wrong. By building trust, you can reduce, if not remove, the fuel for their blame. The more trust you build with such people early on, the more apt they will be to show flexibility, patience, and good humor when needed.

- *Head toward trouble.* You can't build trust with people if you don't spend time with them. Take on the personal challenge of heading toward, not away from, the difficult people in your group. On trips, share your break times with people you think might cause trouble, such as Dan and Nora.
- *Find nonthreatening ways to start a dialogue.* Get to know the people who oppose, or might oppose, you. Share personal experiences on issues of common interest: jobs, families, hobbies. Talk about your sport and the trip you're on. Listen to what the others have to say.

I was once on a three-person county panel to make recommendations on wetlands protection. I represented the environmental community. My partners were the county planning director and a big-time land use consultant. All three of us had tangled before. The only common ground we could find initially was sports. Talking about sports for a half-hour settled us down, confounded some ugly stereotypes we all had assumed, and let us get to know each other a little better. During our next meeting, with our dukes now held lower, we discovered that all of us understood the importance of wetlands in much the same way, and that none of us, as property owners, wanted land use laws to be any more onerous than they had to be.

- *Remember that the key to building trust is caring.* Show your opponents that you genuinely care about them. Listen to what they tell

you; try to put yourself in their shoes. Go out of your way to acknowledge their strengths. Because difficult people are, well, difficult, they often have few friends; they will appreciate caring moves
from you even if they don't show their feelings.

■ *Take a trip into the "iceberg."* If you know or learn of some issue
buried in an opponent's iceberg, look for a sensitive and caring
way in which to bring it up. For example, if you know that Dan
was just passed up for a promotion he expected at work, and that
he's seething at the injustice he perceives, find a way to talk about
that. Start perhaps by talking about work in general, and then
comment about some similar disappointment in your own work
life. The discussion may help defuse some of the explosive emotions Dan feels around that issue, emotions that are spilling over
into other parts of his life, including rafting.

■ *Do simple favors.* I'm always amazed at the power of simple favors
to build trust with difficult people. "Hey, Nora, can I fill your
canteen?" could be seven of the most important words you'll utter
that day. Nora doesn't have a history of people doing her favors,
and her feelings around that fuel her defensiveness. Even a gesture
as small as offering to fill her canteen could change her mood.

■

"Here's your crew list, Suzanne, get going." That was all the fire dispatch
officer said to me before I headed out the door to lead ten people on a
wildland fire-fighting assignment. Quickly reviewing the crew list, I saw
that, including myself, there were four women and seven men of varying
ages and experience levels. Three of the men on the crew had been
working together on a chainsaw crew for two months, they were eighteen to twenty years old and had no previous fire experience. Ed was
their boss; he was my senior in age but not experience. Two people on
the crew warned me that Ed had wanted to lead this crew. According
to their story, Ed had stormed out of the dispatch office saying it was an
insult to be working for "a little girl."

Before gathering the crew together, I decided that I first needed to
talk with Ed. I asked him to help me get things ready, and we chatted a
bit. I asked him if he would head-up the saw crew, and said I looked
forward to having his experience on the crew. Although he was civil, he
was clearly angry. I was disappointed that I wasn't able to break the ice,
and I had the feeling that I was now the focus of an attitude of resentment that had been brewing for years.

As soon as we arrived at the fire, Ed's squad became a problem. If I
spoke, they would look at Ed or glare at me; if I assigned them a task,
they wouldn't move until Ed gave them the go-ahead. Ed's squad's

refusal to pay attention to me was dangerous and threatened to divide the group. After several attempts to find common ground and lighten their mood I had gotten nowhere. Unfortunately, I didn't have the luxury of ignoring their behavior; I was responsible for their safety and they were inexperienced. To make matters worse I was struggling with feelings of anger and resentment of my own; I was tired of being judged by people that didn't know me. I was very angry at Ed for taking out years of frustration on me and encouraging unprofessional behavior in his crew. My fear for their safety and desire for a successful team effort helped me move things forward.

It wasn't until the fire blew up and made a run for our line that Ed and his crew looked me in the eye and listened to instructions. As the fire raged and they saw me remain calm, work hard, care for their health and safety, and encourage teamwork, they followed my lead. At the same time, my respect for them grew as they worked hard under unfamiliar and difficult conditions.

By the time the fire was out, Ed and his crew were still cool toward me. Although we hadn't settled our differences, we had found common ground, respect, and trust through hard work and accomplishment.
—Suzanne Hanlon, Tours Director, Adventure Cycling Association

If conflict starts, take advantage of whatever trust you've built to calmly and carefully look for easy fixes. Focus on the kinds of creative, common sense options that are easily missed when people—including you—get swept up in the emotions of the moment.

Continuing the example that began this chapter—Devil's Fork is the last section on the Roughwater River of your trip. Your vehicles are parked only a short paddle from where both forks smooth out again. There's plenty of time left. One of the beginners could drive you, Dan, Nora, and one raft back up above the fork, so that the three of you could try the more adventurous route. The rest of the crew could either wait, sunning themselves on the rocks below the fork, or start the drive home, leaving one vehicle for the three of you.

Sounds easy, but this is exactly the kind of option that is most often missed when tempers flare.

There's one serious caution in looking for "easy fixes," however: be wary of conventional compromises that simply "split the difference." This tactic will do more harm than good if it shoves unresolved issues under the rug to avoid a conflict. The issues are sure to erupt later.

A developer sees a local wetland as soggy ground that needs to be drained and converted into "something useful." An environmentalist thinks the wetland shouldn't be touched. Weary of fighting, they agree to fill half the wetland. None of their underlying principles are aired. Nasty skirmishes break out around every minor element of the compromise, poisoning the atmosphere further and ensuring that the same battle will continue to erupt.

If easy fixes aren't possible, make sure both sides know what they're fighting about.
- *Outline the differences as accurately as you can.* Explain the rationale for your position, honestly and completely. Be candid about any uncertainties or downsides you see in your position and be open about your feelings, as a way of inviting others to respond in kind. Be equally clear, if you're the leader, that you're uniquely responsible for the safety and well-being of the group, and that this responsibility will affect the positions you take.
- *Acknowledge others' responses and seek any needed clarifications.* If you sense the other side is being less than candid, respectfully ask questions until you're satisfied that everybody knows what the differences really are.

  On the Roughwater River, for example, there are two substantive differences: whether or not the left fork is as dangerous as you think; and whether or not beginners could perform effectively on it.
- *Don't moralize.* If your opponents feel defensive, which they probably do, moralizing will make them dig in for sure. The more you're able to focus the fight on the key substantive differences, the less likely it will be to veer off into the kind of moralizing that creates real battles. Once Nora screams "You're chicken!" and you call her irresponsible, your problem is going to be much harder to solve.
- *Get more information.* Look for any sources that might shed light on the key differences you've uncovered. If you meet another party that has just rafted down the left fork, for example, you could get definitive knowledge of how rough the water is, and that might settle the conflict. This kind of breakthrough is rare—but it can happen.

Begin exploring for common ground, then build on it. Every minute engaged in respectful communication builds trust, as well as further defines the issue.

- *Acknowledge those elements of the others' positions that you do agree with.* "Dan, believe me, I'd love to go down the left fork today, if we could. It'd be one helluva ride."
- *Look for other common goals,* even very general ones such as avoiding accidents. "Nora, I know neither one of us wants this day to end up in a hospital waiting room."
- *Find a way to bring up any shared background or experiences.* Perhaps you took the basic river course with Dan eight years ago. Or maybe Nora and you are the only club members to have ever rafted in Alaska.
- *Ask the other(s) what they would do if they were in your shoes,* with your responsibilities. Would Dan and Nora *really* risk taking beginners down the left fork if they were responsible for the safety of all twelve people?

With each element of common ground you discover, emotions dampen, trust rises, and the situation moves a little further from "you against me" toward "you and me against the problem." Picture yourself with your opponents, standing within the shared area of several intersecting circles, each representing a set of values and priorities. Your objective now is to work together to expand that shared area, by finding and acknowledging additional common ground.

Create new options. This mutual search for what brings you together, as opposed to what sets you apart, creates an atmosphere in which all sides will find it easier to use their energy and imagination to create options that were not possible or could not be seen before in a climate charged with suspicion and anger. People become more receptive to ideas and insights, no matter who suggests them.

Take advantage of this more constructive and trusting atmosphere, first, by reviewing every element of common ground you've discovered.

In the Roughwater River story, for example, the three of you agree that the left fork would be a great run; that safety issues are very important; and that the best trip down the left fork would be in a raft with four experienced people, so nobody would have to worry about anyone panicking, falling out, or failing to paddle well. The three of you also agree that you, as designated leader, have responsibilities the others don't. And while it might not be expressed, it's also clear that nobody wants the inevitable hassles within the club that would result if this dispute is not resolved.

With this common ground now clear to everyone, and with emotions damped and some trust created by the process that got you this far—your task as leader now is to encourage fresh thinking. Ask if anyone sees any new options for the decision you must make. Acknowledge any new insights and suggestions. If a promising new option does emerge, keep talking about it, adding details, examining objections, and gradually getting all the parties interested and excited in it. If/when there's agreement, then assign responsibilities and commit yourselves to carrying out the new option—together.

In conventional "win/lose" negotiations, this tactic might be considered foolish; here, it's a powerful way to reach solutions that serve all sides. If you've managed to bring the process to this point, people should now begin to see themselves less as proponents of a side than as allies working together to solve a common problem. Sometimes the most crucial move for you as leader at this point is to spot and suggest face-saving outs that could make it easier for people to climb down off earlier, strongly-held positions.

Nora shrugs, and points out that it's almost certain that high water conditions will continue for at least another two weeks. What if, she asks, the three of you came back up in a week and ran the left fork by yourselves?

You tell her that that sounds like a great idea, and that you're free the next weekend. You add that it would be particularly fun to take on this challenge with her and Dan, since the three of you, because you're all instructors, rarely get to be in the same raft.

It turns out that Dan is also free. With the option Nora has suggested now a real possibility, the three of you now discuss additional details to make sure it can happen. For example, Dan adds that it should be easy to enlist a fourth expert rafter from the club, once you tell people how the water is running through Devil's Fork. Maybe you could even fill two rafts with experienced people.

With this second trip now set, the three of you now agree that the group you've got now should finish this trip on as high a note as possible. Taking the beginners down the easier water in the right fork will be an exciting challenge for them—and sharing their excitement could be a lot of fun for the "pros" too.

And if this strategy doesn't work? Sometimes the issues on the table are truly intractable. Sometimes the issues beneath the water line of your opponent's iceberg are simply too deep and too powerful, and even the best efforts can't build enough trust to proceed with this strategy.

If this is the case, quietly and firmly reaffirm that, as leader, you bear ultimate responsibility—and have final say—for decisions made on the trip. If anyone then insists on leaving the group and you think this is unwise, formally state your opposition in front of a witness.

Play the odds. A strategy of building trust doesn't work every time. But it will consistently raise your odds of success in dealing with conflict of any kind.

It's ironic that this strategy of building trust is sometimes considered idealistic. I've seen the process work far too often to believe this. To me, the idealists are those who think that the old win/lose approaches to conflict are going to work at all, despite years and sometimes decades of watching them fail.

Many who refuse to even try a trust-building approach are reluctant, not because they think it won't work, but because they are afraid to try. They have a point. The caring, trusting, and sometimes vulnerability, demanded by this approach ask far more from your spirit and character than does squaring off to fight. It's your choice.

Resolving Conflicts

❑ **Remember: you're in charge of how you respond,** no matter what the provocation.

❑ **Be aware of preformed judgments** you may have of your opponents. Hanging onto these beliefs creates self-fulfilling prophecies and undermines your chances for success.

❑ **Understand that the real issues driving any conflict are rarely the obvious ones.** Any conflict is like an iceberg with seven-eighths of its mass below the water line.

❑ **The key to success in dealing with conflict is to build trust between you and your opponent(s).**

❑ **If you sense there are difficult people along, go out of your way early to open dialogues and take actions that build trust.**

  ■ *Head toward trouble.* Spend time with the difficult people in your group.

  ■ *Find nonthreatening ways to start a dialogue.*

  ■ *Remember that the key to building trust is caring.*

  ■ *Take a trip into the iceberg.* Look for appropriate ways to bring up sensitive issues as a way of defusing some of the emotions around them.

  ■ *Do simple favors.*

❑ **If conflict starts, take advantage of whatever trust you've built to calmly and carefully look for easy fixes.** But don't shove important issues under the rug to avoid a conflict.

❑ **If easy fixes aren't possible, make sure both sides know what they're fighting about.**

  ■ *Outline the differences as accurately as you can.*

  ■ *Acknowledge others' responses and seek any needed clarifications.*

  ■ *Don't moralize.*

  ■ *Get more information.*

❑ **Begin exploring for common ground, then build on it.**

  ■ *Acknowledge those elements of the others' positions that you do agree with.*

  ■ *Look for other common goals.*

  ■ *Find a way to bring up any shared background or experiences.*

  ■ *Ask the other(s) what they would do if they were in your shoes.*

❑ **Create new options.** Take advantage of the more constructive and trusting atmosphere you've created by reviewing the common ground you've found, then asking for fresh options that might have been missed earlier. If/when you find one that all parties can agree to, flesh it out, then assign responsibilities and commit yourselves to carrying it out.

❑ **And if this strategy doesn't work?** Reaffirm that, as leader, you bear ultimate responsibility—and have final say—for decisions made on this trip.

❑ **Play the odds**. A strategy of building trust doesn't work every time. But it will consistently raise your odds of success in dealing with conflict of any kind.

Chapter Thirteen

Dealing with Stress

The key to dealing with stress is to lessen the perception that you're trapped—that there's no way out. Mapping out a set of moves tells your mind and emotions that there is a way out—and that you've found it.

This chapter focuses on the small-scale misfortunes, conflicts, and delays that are responsible for 90 percent of the stresses most of us face on a regular basis in the outdoors. The stresses we tend to remember, however, are the other 10 percent.

We'd been climbing since early morning on Grand Teton under clear blue Wyoming skies. The rock was firm, with the kind of generous holds that make even the least skillful of climbers feel strong and graceful. A few hundred feet short of the summit, we inched up a 20-foot chimney to a small snowfield pasted on the mountain's flank.

It was then that the first dark cloud appeared, scudding directly over the summit from the west, then two clouds, then three. In five minutes the entire sky was dark and a wind that meant harm began to blow.

Coming from Seattle, we all were used to storms. But this time a strange buzzing filled the air, like radio static. I looked over at Allen, who was pointing back at me. His hair was standing straight up. Small tongues of blue flame jumped from the tip of his ice ax.

"Get rid of metal!" yelled Steve behind me. He had climbed in these mountains before. "Fast!"

Quickly we stripped off our climbing hardware, and put all of it,

136

along with our ice axes and crampons, in a pile in the snow 20 feet away. Still, static buzzed in our ears, as if coming directly from our bodies. "Hug the ground!" yelled Steve. "Get yourself as low as you can!"

Thunder now boomed all around us, and the first flashes of lightning forked from the dark sky.

We spread-eagled ourselves in the snow. Hailstones the size of gumballs began to pelt us, the bigger ones hitting with enough force to leave bruises. I'd been climbing in a T-shirt, and after a couple of minutes with my body pressed in the snow, I began to shake uncontrollably from the cold. My parka was lying only a few feet away, on the rock where I'd left it. I raised my head and arm to grab it. "Don't!" yelled Steve.

It was too late. That small movement focused the electricity around me. I got my head down fast enough so that the bolt missed me and struck a large boulder 10 feet away. The rock was wrapped in fire, tongues of flame arcing in all directions. A thunderous boom rocked the mountain, deafening us. I buried my face as deep in the snow as I could, and forgot about my parka.

In five minutes it was over. The clouds blew past almost as suddenly as they had appeared. Slowly, carefully, we pried ourselves out of the snow, checking to see that we were all alive and unhurt. We gathered our wits, dug our equipment out from under a blanket of hailstones, and continued on to the top of the best lightning rod for 200 miles in any direction.

For me, that was an unforgettable moment of stress. To this day I can't see a lightning sky without remembering how that Teton rock looked, bathed in blue flame.

None of us forget life-threatening situations, nor the stress they produce.

- Your belay anchor pulls out with the leader hanging by her fingers 40 feet above your head;
- You swing around a patch of blueberries on your favorite trail and suddenly find yourself between a grizzly and her two cubs;
- You're skiing when you hear a dull crack and feel a sudden settling; you realize that an avalanche is starting under your feet.

No matter how unforgettable these dangerous moments may be, however, it's my experience that stress caused by physical danger is not the hardest kind to handle. For one thing, instinctive survival mechanisms embedded in our genetic code instantly start to work when our lives and safety, or the lives and safety of others close to us, are threatened. Adrenaline pumps, and we react—often with amazing effectiveness. For another, in most of the situations that threaten your life in the outdoors, you rarely have enough time to think about what's going on. Stress builds on itself, and in fast-moving physical situations there's seldom enough time for thinking. The lightning—the fall—the bear—the avalanche—will either get you or not, and none of it will take very long.

Stress caused by physical danger is also rare, if only because most of us don't often run into the situations that can cause it. We climb, we ski, we run rapids—but nearly all of the time with enough control so that we don't feel that our lives are on the line.

The situations that stress us most often are a lot less dramatic than those singular moments when we're faced with a cosmic shake of the dice. Sometimes, it seems that it's the very ordinariness of the situation that makes the stress so hard to take.

- A rainstorm catches you 3 miles from the trailhead. Several obnoxious beginners are blaming you for not having started down sooner. Meanwhile, the seam you forgot to seal in your parka is letting a cold stream of water drizzle down the back of your neck.
- You're in charge of setting up a new crevasse rescue training course. Half the people who offered to help have backed out. You're running out of time and the details are driving you crazy.
- You're banquet chair and the invitations come back printed upside down two days before they have to be mailed.
- You find yourself in a messy conflict over whether or not to turn around on a snowshoe hike. You're concerned that if you go on, you'll run out of daylight before you get back to the cars. Jeff and Linda are adamant about continuing. Other people are yelling at each other.

Fill in your own blanks with the kinds of situations that cause *you* stress most often. Some of them may be physical encounters. Some of them certainly stem from conflicts, or from impossible deadlines. Think of the nasty or incompetent people with whom you sometimes have to deal. And think of all the little, inconsequential things that somehow still seem to always rattle your cage. The strategy outlined below will help you through. Pick a choice example or two and follow along.

Take a deep breath. The first step in dealing with any kind of stress is to quiet your emotions enough so that you can begin to evaluate your situation and the moves you need to make. Do a spiritual or mind-centering exercise. Count to ten. Take a long walk. Keep doing it until you feel those little needles of panic start to flatten out.

That grizzly bear is as scared as you are; make a sudden wrong move and she'll kill you. You need to remember what you know about bear encounters. But you can't remember if you're panicked. Don't move, and take five seconds to calm down enough to figure out your next move.

When things really get tense right before a big rescue, I clean coffee cups. The old-timers used to say to smoke a cigarette to calm yourself before you head out; if it was a really big deal, then smoke two!

But that was then. Now, if we have to start organizing a major rescue, I'll take a few minutes to clear off the table in our office. Then I'm ready to get out the checklists, make the plans, and head out. I'm known for this. People say, "Well, Tim must be pretty wired up today—he just cleaned four cups."

—Tim Auger, Public Safety Specialist,
Search and Rescue, Banff National Park

Be here now. Asking "Why is this happening to me?" or thinking "What rotten luck!" are dangerous responses to a stressful situation. The more time and focus you spend wishing you were somewhere else, the less you have of both for dealing with the situation in front of you. Facing that bear, every second you spend bemoaning your fate is a second lost for figuring out how to save your skin.

And if the source of your stress is human, blaming other people for their failures offers no release from stress, but the reverse. The more you blame the people stressing you, the less likely it is that they will act in ways to relieve the stress. Tuck in your anger or disappointment until you've dealt with the situation at hand; you can always straighten accounts with others later.

You had no idea that Jeff and Linda could become this nasty over a disagreement. The two of them are backing you into a corner in front of the entire group, making you very uncomfortable.

So it's uncomfortable. The fact is, it's your job to figure out what to do. Telling Jeff and Linda what you think of them now would really create a brawl, just when everybody needs to think clearly. You can settle with them back in the city. Meanwhile, deal with the situation at hand.

> If I'm feeling stressed, I find something that I like to do, and I do it. And if the stress is due to some disagreement, I just put that behind me. Never brood. You can't change what's already gone. I don't ever think about what might have been.
> —Paul Petzoldt, founder of the National Outdoor Leadership School

Don't question your own competence to deal with the situation. Whatever skills, knowledge, and experience you have—or don't have— are the cards you have for the hand that now must be played. Sure, you might be able to improve these factors for the next round—but that won't help you now.

Play these cards as well as you can. If you doubt your own ability to handle the situation, you'll undermine your capacity to perform at or above your best. Better to move in the other direction. Remind yourself of the skills, knowledge, and experience you do have, and use these reminders to reinforce your faith in meeting the challenge successfully.

These people are blaming you for them getting wet because you started the team down the trail so late. You know they're going to get a lot wetter before they get to the cars. You sure wish you'd remembered to seal the seam in your parka, but there's not much you can do about that now, either.

But wait a minute. It's not like this is the most uncomfortable moment you've ever had to live through. What you have to do now is to get everyone, including yourself, in better moods for one more hour. You can do that; you've done it before. People keep telling you you have a great sense of humor—well, here's a test.

Remind yourself that you're in control of your own emotional responses. No matter how bad you may feel, stress is caused not by the outside provocations themselves, but by your emotional responses to them, responses you can control. Confirming to yourself that you *do* have a choice of how you'll respond emotionally will increase the likelihood of responding welling—and that will lower your stress.

The banquet invitations are printed upside down. What you feel like doing is calling the printer and screaming at him. You've got every right to do that—how could he have made such a stupid mistake? If you do scream at him, however, you're going to increase both his stress level and your own. He'll botch up the invitations again, or tell you to take your business elsewhere, and you'll go crazy for sure. There will be plenty of time later to let him know how you feel about his mistake. Meanwhile there's a big problem here; if you stay cool, maybe you can solve it.

Look for an easy fix. If the phone is ringing off the hook, unplug it. If you're faced with an overwhelming number of tasks, do the first two. The printer who botched those invitations works Saturdays. Call him right now. There's still time for him to redo the job.

Make a plan. Nothing compounds stress more than the feeling that you're trapped. If no easy fix can rid you of your stress, mapping out a set of moves tells your mind and emotions that there *is* a way out and that you've found it.

If you've made contingency plans or in another way have anticipated the stressful situation you're now in, remind yourself now of the moves you planned.

■

In general, if I'm feeling stressed, I go for walks. I look at flowers. I listen to the wind. I lose myself in the wilderness.

In a crisis on a mountain, I slow down and assess my options. Then I carefully think through the steps I want to take and the order in which I want to take them. I get everybody else on the team as calm as I can; then I set them to work on making things happen. I talk in a soothing voice, and I touch people.

—Laura Evans, President/CEO,
Expedition Inspiration and author, *The Climb of My Life*

■

You knew that some of the people who had offered to help you organize the crevasse rescue training course would back out—that's why you enlisted a half-dozen more than the minimum you figured you'd need. The club's monthly meeting is tomorrow night, and there should be plenty of potential volunteers in attendance. Get on the agenda so you can make a strong pitch for additional hands. The biggest gap is one more person who's really good at rigging pulley rescue systems. Lynn told you three months ago that she'd help if you got into a bind. Well, you're in a bind—call her up.

If you have no plan ready, take the time to create one. Think out the moves you need to make.

You're following Mary up a steep cliff face. She rigged the belay anchor securing you to the cliff and now it has pulled out just as she's starting her crucial move on an unprotected traverse above your head. Call up to her to stop her from moving. Tell her what's happened with the anchor and ask her to hold her position until you can fix it. Meanwhile, you're scanning the rock behind you. Looks as if Mary chose a metal chock one size too small. You've got the right size on the rack hanging from your shoulder. The plan is to ease the correct chock off your rack, then replace the small chock with the larger one, then re-secure the rope as fast as you can. Meanwhile, keep your body balanced so that if you have to, you can take her fall without the anchor.

Make a move to start implementing your plan. The instant you make the first move in your plan, you'll start to create a sense of forward momentum. You'll feel more competent, less trapped, and less stressed.

Deal with long-term stress by creating your own challenge. If no quick fixes are possible and it's clear you're going to have to live with this stressful condition for some time, then how you perceive the situation becomes even more crucial.

Stress is often caused, and is certainly made worse, by the perception that you're trapped, that events are beyond your control. Naturally, you don't like the idea of being trapped, and you resist—for example, by complaining about faithless friends, fickle weather, or broken equipment. When your complaints don't improve the situation, your perception of being trapped only increases—and so does the stress.

An effective strategy for dealing with stress, especially when caused by situations that can't be shifted quickly or easily, is to work on your perception of being trapped.

Do this by creating a challenge-within-a-challenge. Come up with a test set in the same stressful situation you started with, but with goals and objectives that you create yourself. The function of this second, self-imposed challenge is to move your attention away from the original challenge—the one that has you feeling so trapped—to one on which you can make some progress, and on your own terms. Three examples of a challenge-within-a-challenge are inventing your own game, challenging your own spirit, and improving the experiences of others.

Invent your own game.

Before you can run that crevasse rescue course successfully, you figure you're going to need eight more assistants, not counting Lynn, the pulley-rigging expert. So you make eight marks on the wall next to your phone, or you draw a picture of a bridge over a crevasse that takes eight steps to cross, and you move a stick figure across the bridge as people sign up. Sure, it's a game, but it focuses your attention onto goals that you've set yourself, while diverting your attention away from the time pressures created by schedules that aren't within your control.

Challenge your own spirit.

Back on that snowshoe hike with Jeff and Linda, challenge yourself to use a trust-building strategy for handling the conflict, no matter how hard that gets. Can you take a deep breath instead of returning their fire? Can you put yourself in Jeff and Linda's shoes enough to really care about what's driving them? Can you find enough common ground to get them to join you in a calmer search for options? Can you hold your temper despite all their provocations?

The facts of the conflict with Jeff and Linda are unchanged. It's your perception of it that has shifted, and that makes all the difference. As long as you see the situation as "I'm faced with two nasty, immovable people who are driving me nuts," Jeff and Linda are in control and you're going to feel trapped. But if you see the same situation as "Let's see how good I am at building trust with really difficult people," you create an exciting challenge to your own spirit, one in which you set the goals and you measure the progress.

Improve the experiences of others who are in the same stressful situation as you, but who may be having a worse time dealing with it.

On that rainy hike, what if you challenge yourself to get every single one of those miserable people to laugh before they reach their cars? You're going to have to be very creative and funny to accomplish this. And, of course, you'll have to flip yourself out of your own bad mood first. So what'll it be? An increasingly grim march down the soggy trail, or every bad pun, outrageous joke, and stupid game and song you can think of? What'll it take to get these people to turn one wet hour into a memorably funny experience for all of them?

All three of these challenges-within-a-challenge are defined by you alone. No one is telling you to develop your own system for counting volunteer instructors, or to use a trust-building approach to resolve a conflict, or to make a game of a rainy hike. These are your own decisions, your own yardsticks for measuring progress, not somebody else's.

Start working on your own challenge-within-a-challenge and almost immediately you'll feel your stress level go down. You're not stumped—you're moving. Your focus isn't on the undoables but on meeting a challenge you set, one that has meaning for you.

This doesn't mean that you lose sight, or fall short, of the goals of the original challenge—quite the opposite. As your stress level goes down, you'll find yourself doing a better job with the original challenge because you're calmer, more focused, and more effective. This is true whether the task entails enlisting volunteers, settling a conflict, or getting a bunch of tired, wet people to laugh in the rain.

Get ready for next time. When this current stress has passed, ask yourself what you could do to help better prepare for the next time.

Maybe you need more or better equipment. The threat of avalanches will be reduced, for example, if you and your buddies have avalanche rescue beacons and learn how to use them. Sealing the seam in your parka will at least eliminate one source of stress on wet hikes.

Maybe you should change your cast of characters. There must be another printer in your town who doesn't print invitations upside down. And nobody is making you take people on your trips who you know are nasty and uncooperative.

Think about getting more training. There are plenty of guidebooks on how to deal with bears, for example; before your next hike in bear country you might want to read one.

Most importantly, ask yourself what you learned from the crisis that has just passed. What could you have done or said differently that would have produced even better results? The more you learn from each crisis, the better you'll handle the next one.

Dealing with Stress

❑ **It's the ordinary stuff that stresses us most often.** Stress caused by physical danger is neither the most likely nor the hardest kind to handle.

❑ **Take a deep breath.** Quiet your emotions enough so you can begin to evaluate your situation and the moves you need to make.

❑ **Be here now.** Don't waste time wishing you were somewhere else, or blaming other people for their failures.

❑ **Don't question your own competence.** Play the cards you have as well as you can.

❑ **Remind yourself that you're in control of your own emotional responses.** Confirming to yourself that you do have this choice will increase your confidence and lower stress.

❑ **Look for an easy fix.**

❑ **Make a plan.** If no easy fix exists, mapping out a set of moves tells your mind and emotions that there's a way out and that you have found it. Pull up any contingency plans already made.

❑ **Make a move** to implement your plan, and you'll start to create a sense of forward momentum.

❑ **Deal with long-term stress by creating your own challenge-within-a-challenge.** Refocus your attention away from the original challenge—the one that has you feeling so trapped—to one in which the goals and objectives are set by you. For example:

- *invent your own game;*
- *challenge your own spirit;*
- *improve the experiences of others who are in the same stressful situation as you, but who may be having a worse time dealing with it.*

❑ **Get ready for next time.** Improve your equipment, change the cast of characters you deal with, and/or get additional training. The more you learn from each crisis, the better you'll handle the next one.

Chapter Fourteen

Organizational Leadership

It's inevitable, if you lead outdoors trips long enough, that you'll be asked to take on leadership roles within the organizations to which you belong. Do it. Leading organizations is a natural outgrowth of the skills and experience you've gained from leading in the field.

There's more to keep track of in leading organizations than in leading outdoor trips, including longer-term issues involving values, laws, politics, and the future of the organizations themselves. There are also more people to think about, and greater challenges of communication and planning.

On the other hand, many of the leadership skills that serve you well in the outdoors—such as team building, planning, resolving conflict, and communicating—will be just as useful when you're leading an entire club. Other elements of leadership may be even more useful, or useful in expanded ways, when you're holding office. You're the keeper of the organization's vision, momentum, and values, for example. You're the place where the buck stops when there's a crisis. Your job includes identifying, training, and maintaining the quality of the club's leaders, and promoting the importance of leadership issues. You also need to be able to run a good meeting, keep track of paper, and know when it's time to move on.

■

There are similarities between leading outdoors and leading an organization, but they don't fit into an easy package. Many of the qualities needed in a leader are the same in both situations—imagination, respect, empathy, and the ability to inspire—yet the scale and complexity of an organization can make it quite different. What comes to mind as an analogy is the difference between a four-person bluegrass band and an orchestra. The bluegrass band is usually led by one of the players and, while the music is complex (and satisfying to me), there are only four people in close proximity playing related instruments. An orchestra may have eighty musicians playing a long and complicated piece in which it is important that people do their parts, and it usually takes a full-time conductor who does not even play an instrument to make the thing work. The conductor is the leader of an organization. You must get people to do specific and specialized parts, make their parts meaningful to them, and yet get the whole thing to sound right once it is put together. You must understand the vision and values of the organization and encourage and empower people to translate them with their superior individual skills. The bluegrass leader is getting folks on the same page, too, but she's part of the band and only has to worry about three others.

Organizations are conceptual; trips, more concrete. What I love about expeditions is that they are contained and focused. You need to deal with food, clothing, shelter, and an objective that stretches but doesn't exceed the physical capabilities of the group. Out of doors, everything is simpler and more real, concrete. I feel refreshed from that simplicity and from the fact that trips have a beginning and an end, a time to anticipate and a time to reflect and tell tales. Organizations are ongoing; as the leader you have to help establish those psychic rewards and times to pause and reflect. Leading organizations challenges you to remember, from your outdoor experience, what makes for a satisfying journey and bring it into a new medium. Both types of leadership are satisfying and can be mutually enriching, and both benefit tremendously from a sense of humor and good luck.

—Sally McCoy, Managing Director, Sierra Designs

■

Keep the flame bright: vision, momentum, and values. If you're leading an organization, you have primary responsibility for keeping the vision for its work sharp, inspiring, and relevant; for maintaining the momentum of its policies and programs; and for defining and upholding its values.

Vision. All significant organizations are created out of compelling visions that communicate their purpose and provide both inspiration and guidance. These visions often stay bright for years, even decades. Inevitably, however, they become stale and lose relevance unless they are renewed.

You've been elected president of your ski club. On the face of it, everything is "working": the books are balanced; the club's cabin has just been remodeled and repaired; and all the committee chairs have agreed to keep serving, some of them for the third or fourth year.

You know, however, that the club's membership has hardly grown in the last several years. There seem to be more complaints every winter that the schedule of club trips remains relentlessly the same. Monthly meetings are poorly attended, guest lectures are mostly boring show-and-tell, and every board meeting you've been to has been a struggle to assemble a quorum. When asked to provide testimony to the state legislature on a new law concerning snowmobiles, your club declined because it couldn't find anybody willing to go. There's little sense of energy or excitement in the club, or anticipation of the future.

What has happened is that the club's vision has died. As leader, your first task is to bring it back to life.

You ask all the club's officers and leaders to attend a special meeting to discuss this challenge. When you broach your concerns, all but a few nod in agreement; several complain that the club "just isn't any fun" any more. When you read the visionary statement in the club's founding documents, people are embarrassed that so little of it seems to apply thirty years later.

Then you take your officers and leaders through a visioning exercise. You ask them to create clear, concrete pictures in their minds of an ideal club, one year in the future. When you ask them to share what they've "seen," a flood of pictures pours out: meetings that are fully attended, sparked by interesting speakers and discussions of cutting-edge issues; a new series of training courses covering the latest topics in backcountry skiing, leadership, and avalanche safety; trips to new and untried slopes; a surge of new members; club officers making the organization's voice known in public policy sessions on issues such as land use, environmental pollution, and use of off-road vehicles; and more.

The excitement in the room builds as more details are added to this renewed vision for the club. When everybody's pictures have been expressed, you and the group spend several hours condensing them into a vision statement, then using that statement as the basis for an updated set of club goals and objectives. When this is done, you send out the newly drafted vision statement, goals, and objectives to every member of the club for comment. You use the feedback to refine, then formally adopt and publish the new documents as the club's inspiration and guidance for the future.

Momentum in policies and programs. The goals and objectives flowing from an organization's vision become the guidance for specific policies and programs, such as trip schedules, training courses, leader qualification standards, meeting topics, and political initiatives. Some of these policies and programs will be updated versions of what already exists; some will express the exciting new pictures created by the club's visioning. All of them will create a forward momentum, a sense of dynamism and anticipation that will create interest, commitment, and support.

It's your job now to follow through, to make sure that the momentum doesn't die, and that the initial excitement doesn't fade. See that the new policies are implemented and that the new programs move off the drawing board. Use club newsletters and meetings to keep people talking about the vision and the new possibilities it presents. Get as many people involved as you can, even in minor roles; the more the members feel they have a stake in what's going on, the more likely they will support and publicize the club.

Values. An organization's vision helps define its values, the qualities of ethics and service that matter to it most. You may, for example, be part of a club with a rich history of environmental activism, or a fine reputation for developing training courses, or a people-centered approach that makes even rank beginners feel comfortable and involved. Out of values such as these flow the principles and standards that help guide the organization's work and shape its reputation.

Your responsibility as leader is to make sure these values are broadly understood, agreed to, and honored by everybody within the organization. The club may have spent decades building a tradition of excellence. In letting people act in its name, it's trusting them to measure up. If that trust is abused, it's up to you to take action.

Just as the momentum of your first year as president of the ski club is starting to build, you discover a serious problem. In remodeling the club cabin the year before, club officers had deliberately failed to observe county health regulations on septic disposal and had falsified the compliance reports. You learn this right before you're about to enroll the club as a member of the state's pre-eminent environmental policy organization.

You call an emergency meeting and point out that this failure is in direct contradiction to the club's vision of itself as a model and leader in environmental protection. The people responsible apologize, but point out that this "shortcut" they took was standard practice for rural buildings in this area, far from county inspectors.

No one, however, contradicts you when you point out that being able to get away with the shortcut is not the issue. The issue is how much integrity is left in the club's vision of itself, and in the values flowing from that vision. If the club's integrity is compromised, the vision can't possibly be successful as either an inspiration or a guide. While the club's reputation with outsiders might not suffer if the shortcut remains secret, it's the members' self-appraisal that really counts—and that will plummet.

The county shuts down the cabin for an entire winter. The club has to pay $1,000 in fines and another $4,000 in reconstruction costs. When it's all over, however, there's a pleasing sense of pride in what the club has done. The initial story in the newspaper is embarrassing, but follow-up stories praising the club for "doing the right thing," and "being a model" more than make up for the initial damage.

You as leader of an organization must be alert to transgressions against its values. Your primary role is not to police, however, but to ensure that the organization has a self-policing mechanism that regularly audits its own values. It's your job to oversee that process, to make sure that no reports are ignored, and that abuses and mistakes are corrected.

Finally, it's also your job to make sure that the organization's values don't become mere slogans. Insist that your organization, at least once a year, takes time to look hard at its values, examining them for their continuing relevance and redefining and/or clarifying them as necessary.

Stop the buck. A sign on Harry Truman's desk proclaimed "The Buck Stops Here." You don't have to be president of the country to appreciate the wisdom of that advice to organizational leaders. How you act as leader, especially if there's trouble, sets the tone for how your entire organization will respond, and does more than anything else to determine the outcome.

You've been president of your kayaking club for two months when one of your members drowns in a tragic accident on a club trip. You've been told by the trip leader that the accident was unavoidable, a freak occurrence—but the local newspaper asks to interview you and the reporter mentions something about possible negligence on the part of the club. You call an emergency meeting of your governing board, but, when they collect, most of them seem more concerned with avoiding personal legal liability then anything else.

At that meeting, you need to do three things:
■ control your own emotions and prepare yourself internally to handle the crisis;

- calm your board members, using your own example to inspire them to be at their best; and
- make and implement a plan.

Control your emotions. Prepare yourself internally by reminding yourself of the reasons why you took on leadership challenges in the first place. As discussed in Chapters Two and Ten, the degree to which leadership *means* something to you—that it fits in with your deepest ideals and values—is crucial to your effectiveness in dealing with leadership challenges.

Calm others. Your board members are looking to you, not only for policy guidance but also as a model of how to act personally in this crisis. Be conscious of that role. *You're the leader here, not "one of the gang"*—and your people need and want you to act that way.

Even if time is limited, use some of it to help your people create a vision of your club (and them) successfully handling this challenge. Get them to see themselves doing what they have to do, coolly and effectively, before they have to do it: Jack sees himself dealing with the sheriff's department; Paul is with the next-of-kin; Molly is handling all the legal issues; and you're speaking to the press. It's this vision of competency, combined with the model provided by your behavior, that will inspire everyone to be at their best.

Make and implement a plan. The visioning will also suggest practical roles and steps needed to deal with the problem (such as Jack dealing with the sheriff). Add details to these pictures, establish priorities, shape a plan for action, assign responsibilities—and then begin to carry out the plan.

Making a plan and setting it in motion not only confronts the challenge, it also reduces stress. Mapping out a set of moves, as discussed in Chapter Thirteen, tells your mind and emotions that there *is* a way out and that you've found it. Your whole board will feel less trapped and more competent to handle what's in front of them.

Take charge of leadership issues. As leader of an organization, you're responsible for creating and maintaining a sufficient number of trained leaders, and for ensuring their quality. It's also your job to promote the importance of leadership and leadership training in the club.

▪

I'd say that one of the most important responsibilities of people who lead outdoors organizations is to be ethical about training. That is, they must make sure that people get the training they need to go into the outdoors safely. There are so many little things leaders of organizations can do to improve training. If they did them all, it would probably cut accidents by 50 percent.
—Paul Petzoldt, founder of the National Outdoor Leadership School

▪

Make sure your organization has a sound process for identifying, encouraging, training, and developing future leaders. This should include providing a range of courses and refresher courses, covering both technical and leadership skills. The goal is to create a self-renewing cadre of skilled and committed men and women leaders to fill all the club's existing and prospective needs.

Maintain and improve the quality of leadership at all levels. Closely tied to the issue of training and developing leaders is the issue of maintaining their quality. Too many people report that the reason they quit their outdoors clubs was the incompetence of the club leaders they encountered on their first or second trip. They cite lack of technical skills, but more often complain of a lack of "people" skills on the part of leaders who seemed to be leading out of a sense of *machismo* or an overblown ego, who lacked basic techniques in communication, or who seemed to have little caring or sense of responsibility for the people in their groups.

Declining membership is not the worst thing that can happen if club leaders ignore their responsibilities to ensure good leadership. They are also asking for accidents and lawsuits. It's vital that any outdoors organization have in place:

- an effective system for qualifying, retaining, and assigning leaders. This system should be graduated, with people qualified to lead at a series of levels of difficulty, and with rigorous procedures for certifying leaders as ready for the next level. All certifications should have time limits. If a leader doesn't lead a certain number of trips at that level within a certain time, then he or she must requalify. Regular refresher courses should also be mandatory, as they are now for CPR;
- a mentoring system that allows new leaders to "fly copilot" with more experienced leaders until they are ready to move up; and
- an open and fair mechanism for addressing and acting on complaints.

Promote the importance of leadership and leadership training. Organizations tend to shy away from putting leadership on their formal and informal agendas. This is a mistake, because it decreases the likelihood that those organizations will ever provide formal leadership training, and virtually guarantees continuing problems with both quality and quantity of leadership. As leader of an organization, it's your job to give the subject of leadership the prominence in your club that it deserves.

My experience is that most people are not only willing to talk about leadership, including its sensitive elements, they are eager to share their views. They simply need a catalyst—someone to get the conversation going, to demonstrate that talking about leadership is OK.

I was at a ski cabin with a group of friends one evening last winter, and, after an hour of the usual after-dinner chitchat, I thought I'd try to move the conversation to the subject of leadership. Since everybody there was an experienced leader, I went right to the bottom line: I asked everybody whether or not they thought leading in the outdoors had made their lives more meaningful. A few people looked at me as if I'd just crossed a taboo, but others were quick to offer views that they'd obviously been thinking about for a long time. Bob said that the tests of leading in the outdoors seemed a whole lot more real to him than those he tackled as a lawyer. Susan saw leading in the outdoors as a natural extension of her generally forceful, take-charge personality. Robert said that leading in the outdoors was one of the biggest personal challenges he'd ever faced. Soon, the whole group warmed to the conversation, which went on for two hours.

Everybody in the cabin that night learned something, even those who said nothing. And all of us, I think, lost some of the hesitation we used to feel about talking about leadership issues.

By sparking such discussions, you can break an unnecessary silence and open up possibilities for insights and education that will help both you and your colleagues deal with this sometimes sensitive subject.

Carry this same spirit of inquiry into your organization. Make sure your organization includes leadership and leadership training as a regular part of its presentations and publications—for example, a seminar on resolving conflict, a newsletter article on leadership styles, a panel on women in leadership.

Keeping this spirit going will require some commitment from the rest of your club. It's likely that some members will feel that formal presentations on leadership issues wastes time diverted from "real" training challenges such as orienteering and first aid. Hang in there. Changing old paradigms takes time.

Learn to run good meetings. No discussion of organizational leadership is complete without mentioning everybody's least favorite way to warm a chair: the meeting. Nobody wants more meetings then necessary, but well-run meetings are still the best vehicle for getting the right information to the right people in time to be useful, especially if the undertaking is large and complex.

Successful meetings need four ingredients:
- the right people there;
- an agenda;

- time limits;
- an atmosphere of comfort and openness, so that not even the shy-est people in the group are reluctant to speak.

Attendance. The hardest part of a meeting often occurs before the meeting starts: getting the right people in the room. Never rely on posted notices. Single out those people whose presence is absolutely necessary and send written notices or emails, followed up with a phone call.

Agendas don't have to be written down. But everybody needs to know in advance what the purpose of the meeting is. The meeting may well produce some surprises, but the agenda should not be one of them. Any person, however, should be able to ask the group to add items or to change what is already there.

Time limits for individual items and for the meeting as a whole are almost always a good idea, especially if the agenda is large and complex. Time limits not only help ensure that all issues get covered, they also help people focus both their thoughts and their remarks.

Creating an atmosphere of comfort and openness is the step most often left out of meetings that fail. As leader, your first responsibility is to set the tone. No meeting is going to be comfortable and open if you don't model those qualities yourself. You also need to stay closely attuned to he other people there. Especially if it's a regular meeting, you'll know who the shy ones are. You'll know that if Claudia is present, Eric will defer to her and you'll have to coax out what he really thinks. You'll know that sparks almost always fly between Cynthia and Allen, and that the two of them will upset the mood of the meeting unless you act quickly to keep them from jumping on each other's remarks.

There are those who are convinced that physical meetings will be made obsolete by the Internet. I doubt it. At least I've not yet figured out how to inspire people, calm their fears, raise their hopes, ease their suspicions, or show them that I care, by words on a computer screen. Maybe when the day arrives that we can do virtual outdoor trips, we can use virtual meetings to plan them.

Keep good records. It's amazing how vital good records can be to organizations—and how much trouble and pain can be caused when they aren't there. If you're not a details person, then make sure to put someone else you trust firmly in charge of items such as board meeting minutes, lease renewals, audit reports, and the like. In addition, don't forget that, at least for your club, you're making history. Make sure that important events in the life of the club under your watch are documented, and added to the club's archives. Thirty years from now, somebody will want to know.

Know when it's time to leave. The best leaders of organizations have an innate sense of when it's time to move on, when they have maximized their contribution and it's time for somebody else to make theirs. Organizations are constantly in need of renewal, and it's very tough for one person to keep looking at that process in the same organization with fresh eyes. It's inevitable that standard patterns develop. Those patterns may have been brilliant when you created them, and they may have worked well for years. But inevitably there comes a time when something else might work even better—and you may not be the best person to notice it.

If you have been head of an organization for three years or more, and if you sense yourself creating programs for the next year based too much on what worked in the last, it may be time to move on.

And think of yourself, too. Presumably you've learned a lot on the job, and you may be ready for bigger, or at least different, challenges in another organization or part of your life.

Celebrate your departure and, presuming you've done well, make sure your organization celebrates it, too. It's the end of one cycle and the beginning of another—a symbol of healthy growth and change. Both you and your organization have won.

Organizational Leadership

☐ **Keep the flame bright: vision, momentum, and values**. If you're leading an organization:

- *keep the vision for its work sharp, inspiring, and relevant;*
- *maintain the momentum of its policies and programs; and*
- *define and uphold its values.*

☐ **Stop the buck.** How you act as leader, especially if there's trouble, sets the tone for how your entire organization will respond. You need to:

- *control your own emotions;*
- *calm others, using your own example to inspire them to be at their best; and*
- *make a plan and start implementing it.*

☐ **Take charge of leadership issues**.

- *Make sure your organization has a sound process for identifying, encouraging, training, and developing future leaders.*
- *Maintain and improve the quality of leadership at all levels; and*
- *Promote the importance of leadership and leadership training.*

☐ **Learn to run good meetings**. They need four ingredients:

- *the right people there;*
- *an agenda;*
- *time limits; and*
- *an atmosphere of comfort and openness,* so that not even the shyest people in the group are reluctant to speak.

☐ **Keep good records**—board meeting minutes, lease renewals, audit reports, and more.

☐ **Know when it's time to leave**. The best leaders of organizations have an innate sense of when they have maximized their contribution.

Chapter Fifteen

Political Leadership

At its best, politics is how we balance competing interests in a democracy. For many outdoors people, environmental issues are a special focus. Whether you get involved or not—successful politics is about successful leadership.

It makes sense that many outdoors people and outdoors organizations should take on environmental challenges. Logging practices drastically affect forests and streams. Pollution from companies and individuals fouls the water and air. Overcrowding threatens the national parks. Population growth pushes subdivisions farther and farther up into the hills.

The issues and challenges are all too familiar, and they're not going away. Neither government oversight nor corporate conscience can be expected to deal with them effectively. The answer, as it has been since John Muir and the founding of the Sierra Club more than a century ago, is citizen activism.

The core skills needed to lead political initiatives are very much the same as those needed for leading in the outdoors: planning and organizing, caring, building trust, resolving conflict, and creating and communicating a vision.

Still, politics is messy, and it takes considerable time and effort. Most people don't get involved because they want to. They are forced into action because something they value highly is being threatened.

The last time Laura had seen Big Pine Valley, two years before, there'd been waves of tall trees climbing from the valley floor almost to the top of the ridges on either side. Only the top 300 feet of the valley walls were too steep and too rocky for even scraggly pines to grow, and there the trees gave way to cliffs of reddish gray rock. It was not uncommon to see eagles in the highest snags in the valley, and occasionally even a black bear in the lowlands, foraging for berries.

Laura had been leading trips into this area for a decade, and she looked forward to returning to Big Pine. This trip up the valley, however, turned into an ugly surprise. Two miles past Poacher's Bend, a new logging road intersected Big Pine Trail, and just past where the trail crossed Miner's Creek for the first time, Laura suddenly found herself looking at a valley stripped bare of trees. A clearcut extended on both sides of the valley all the way up to the cirque at its head. The sun beat down on the new openness and only the whir of insects gave any distraction to the sudden and unpleasant heat. There were no animals, not even a bird sound.

Laura had never considered herself a "political" person in any way. But now she was mad. One of the prettiest places in the state had been ruined, and for what—sending logs to Japan? Boosting some multinational company's corporate profits? Jamming another subdivision into an overcrowded suburb?

As soon as Laura returned to the city she did something she had never done before: she sent an angry letter to the newspaper which, somewhat to her surprise, published her letter in full. A couple of her friends called to congratulate her. But the next week two rebuttal letters appeared. One of them was from the state's Department of Natural Resources, which owned all the timberland in Big Pine Valley. The DNR letter referred to the cut as "long-planned harvesting" and stated that the Big Pine cut alone would earn over $1.5 million, most of which would go to supporting schools in this impoverished part of the state. And, the letter continued, the logging provided jobs in an area where unemployment hovered above 20 percent.

Another, much nastier, letter was also published. It sneered at "elitist pretty-pants hikers . . . thinking that the outdoors is just their playground . . . when trees are the means of livelihood for the poor families who can't send their kids to college . . . or buy fancy backpacks."

Laura read both letters several times, feeling angry and frustrated by turns. Sure, she'd known about the controversy over logging restrictions and jobs, but she hadn't understood that the harvest of timber on state land was a primary means of supporting rural schools. Still—weren't there other ways to get those funds? Couldn't loggers be employed in other outdoor work? Were clearcuts the only way to log? The situation was much more complex—and volatile—than Laura had thought when she'd fired that first angry blast off to the paper.

Perhaps you've been in Laura's shoes, and felt what she felt after seeing an ugly clearcut in the mountains, sludge floating downriver from a polluting plant, or a park taken over by drug dealers because the city can never "find the funds" to maintain it. It's not enough to say that situations such as these persist because some people profit from them. They also persist because of citizen inertia—because not enough people have risen to challenge them; and because not enough leaders have stepped forward to show the way.

What you need to know to "show the way" is set here in the context of environmental issues, but can just as easily be applied to others:

Getting ready: assessing obstacles and risks, researching, forming a team, finding out who the decision makers are, making a plan, and preparing yourself and your team to deal with conflict.

Getting it done: building trust, probing for buried issues, creating a dialogue with opponents, being street smart, creating a media strategy, avoiding conventional compromises, creating a vision, and moving from vision to policy.

Keeping it done: maintaining the successful structure you've built, and expanding the challenge to other areas of your life.

■

I talked to a group recently who were complaining of all the restrictions we have now on use of the outdoors. I reminded them that these restrictions were imposed because people were over-using and mis-using the wilderness. Instead of complaining, I told them, they should get to work on protecting the environmental assets we have, restoring some that we've lost, and adding new wilderness areas. It's time for global CPR for the environment—conserving, preserving and restoring.

The challenges are enormous, and there's plenty of opposition—but that's nothing new. When the wilderness system we take for granted now was first proposed, private interests opposed it as an infringement of individual rights. But people change. Initially, most people just won't know, or haven't thought enough, about what's going on. But when they see someone showing focus and commitment, many of them will listen, and some of them will change their behavior.

Yes, there are powerful corporations that damage the environment in all kinds of ways. That doesn't mean you can't get them to change too. One corporation, 3M, decided to change, and in fifteen years they cut their contribution to the waste stream by half and increased their profits by half a billion dollars.

Currently, one of the key challenges of change is learning to redesign what we've built. Examples of good redesigns are pull-tabs that no longer separate from drink cans, and one-gallon flush toilets. Our old designs didn't have to take into account environmental consequences. Now they do. Think of three things you personally use that can be redesigned, and work to make that happen.

—David Brower, founder of Earth Island Institute

■

GETTING READY

Look before you leap. Think about the obstacles and risks that may lie ahead. Most political initiatives involve conflicts of one kind or another, and, despite your best efforts, conflicts can get nasty. Political work is often frustrating and stressful—and always involves about twice as much work as you thought. Be prepared for this. Better to not get started, than to get started and back out.

Begin researching the issues. Laura knows that she could have gotten off to a better start if she had read even a little, and made a few telephone calls, before she fired off that first letter.

Laura doesn't have to start her study from scratch. Plenty of other people are concerned with the clearcutting issue and a lot of research has already been done. Laura needs to talk to environmental and public policy groups, for example, including some in other states that have dealt with logging conflicts. If she finds out that another organization is already working hard and well to effect the changes on logging policies that she wants in her state, then the best course for her may simply be to offer her help.

But if that is not the case, and if she has decided to keep going—then she needs to get help.

Form a team around a vision of the results you want. If your issue is even moderately large and complex, don't try to take it on by yourself. Put your initial efforts into forming a team. Start by speaking up at a meeting of your outdoors organization. Put a notice in its newsletter. Get on the phone to your friends.

You'll recruit allies by the strength of your commitment, by the amount of homework you've already done, and by your ideas. But if you don't set your facts into the context of a vision of success, it's doubtful that you'll have the power to sway people to make the kind of commitments you need from them.

Before Laura makes her first calls, she needs to sit quietly and see, as clearly as she can, the picture of what she wants to have happen in places like Big Pine Valley. It's that vision that will add persuasive power to the facts she is gathering.

———

"Ken," Laura might say to an outdoors friend whose help she wants to enlist, "we've got the skills in our club to put together an alternative logging plan that would keep places like Big Pine from getting clearcut, and would do it without undermining local schools and jobs. Jason and you are lawyers. Audrey taught forestry at the university for twenty years. Sam's a state legislator. Nell owns an ad agency. What if we recruit a team of people such as these, come up with a good plan, and then start selling it to environmental organizations, sports fishermen, hunters, the tribes? That'll create a groundswell that the state government can't ignore. All I see out there now on this issue is a lot of tired thinking—we're a fresh voice and we can make a difference."

At the first meeting of the allies she has pulled together, Laura invites everybody to contribute to the vision of what they can do together. Several members of the group, however, see creating a vision as a waste of time. They want to start slaying the dragons right away.

Laura explains that a vision will provide guidance for detailed planning; it will help keep all of them motivated and together; and it will be the most powerful tool they have for convincing others. She asks the doubters to go along with a visioning exercise.

She starts by asking everyone to put themselves three years into the future and to create in their minds clear, concrete pictures of the results they want. She then asks people to share their pictures, reminding them that there's only one rule: they must talk as if they were really looking back from a point three years in the future. They can't use the future tense—no *will*s or *might*s.

The exercise begins slowly and awkwardly, but soon the pictures flow: pristine valleys like Big Pine still covered with trees; other areas logged selectively, with snags and younger trees still standing; rural kids in schools with roofs that don't leak; loggers working at good jobs restoring watersheds and replanting.

When these pictures start to gel in people's minds, Laura asks them to create pictures of what it took to *get* these results—collaborative committees, public forums, individual meetings, lobbying in the state capital, a media campaign—and more.

Within half an hour, a number of good elements are added to Laura's original picture, including, for example, a successful educational effort that creates long-term citizen support for more sensible logging practices; and the involvement of environmental groups in a job creation program for loggers.

Laura writes or draws all these pictures on sheets of butcher paper. Then the group helps her condense them into a few sentences that succinctly express their vision—both for the results they want and the process that will get them there. The vision statement goes like this: "Clearcutting has stopped. Rural schools are well supported. Forest employment is up. The entire process has been win/win, with every stakeholder represented."

Even the doubters get swept up in the process. The group agrees that their vision is attractive, exciting, and doable. While many details remain to be added, the vision is now clear and concrete enough to becomes the basis for a campaign. Laura's team is ready to go.

Find out who the decision makers are. Now Laura's team needs to find out where the key decision-making and decision-shaping power lies, so that its strategies, time, and resources can be targeted toward the people with the most power to make the desired changes.

Who has final say over the actions of the state's Department of Natural Resources, for example? The governor? A special committee? Since the revenues go to schools, how much influence does the state superintendent of public instruction have over logging issues? And what about the logging companies and mills and their associations and lobbies?

What about the politicians? Who are the legislators with the most power to determine natural resource policies on state lands? How partisan is this issue?

Since she started there, Laura is not likely to forget the power of the press—they can do a lot more to sway people than print letters to the editor. Her team needs to find out the editorial policies on this issue of key newspapers and television stations, and who are the key opinion shapers.

Finally, what do various groups of citizens think and feel about clearcutting? Laura has already got some evidence that the rural people around Big Pine don't take too kindly to her position. What do sports fishermen think? Native tribes?

Make a plan. Without a plan, even the most wonderful and visionary of enterprises will quickly collapse into chaos.

Laura makes a wall planning chart out of another long strip of butcher paper. Her group agrees that they should be able to achieve their vision in three years. They draw a horizontal timeline across the planning chart long enough to cover that period (see the example below). Then they write their vision across the top—it will be the basis for all the rest of the planning they'll do.

Now they break down their vision into a set of goals and list these goals along the left side of the chart, leaving plenty of room under each one. Goals for Laura's group might include: changing DNR clearcut policies; maintaining rural school funding; creating rural jobs; educating the public to these issues; and getting legislation passed.

Then Laura's team breaks down each goal into a series of steps and writes these steps under each goal. They show beginning and ending dates for each step by drawing a timeline for each, extending across the chart (see example below). Finally, they put benchmarks on these timelines to mark key events.

———————————

Here is how a simplified version of Laura's planning chart might look. The real chart would have all the steps written in and all the benchmarks, now marked with an asterisk (*), described. It would also be a lot messier, showing finer subdivisions of the work.

LAURA'S PLANNING CHART

The Vision: Clearcutting has stopped. Rural schools are being supported. Forest employment is up. The entire process has been win/win, with every stakeholder represented.

	2008	**2009**	**2010**	**2011**
				completion date
Timeline ————————————————————————————— *				

Goal #1: Change DNR clearcut policies

	benchmark	benchmark		completion date	
Step 1 ___*_____ * _____ *
Step 2_____ * _____ * _____ *
Step 3 _____ * _____ *
etc.

Goal #2: Maintain rural school funding

Step 1_____ * _____ *
Step 2____ * _____ * _____ *
etc.

Goal #3: Create rural jobs

Step 1_____ * _____ *
Step 2____ * _____ * _____ *
etc.

Goal #4: Educate the public to these issues

Step 1_____ * _____ * _____ *
Step 2_____ * _____ *
etc.

Goal #5: Get legislation passed

Step 1 ____*_____ * _____ * _____ *
Step 2 _____ *
Step 3 _____ * _____ * _____ * _____ *
etc.

What's left to do now is assign responsibilities for each part of the action. For big projects, such as Laura's, that probably means forming committees.

Either way, people's names need to be entered on the chart, next to the step or goal for which they have taken responsibility.

This plan is now the guide and schedule for the entire campaign—but that doesn't mean it isn't open to change and refinement. The vision written across the top serves as a check for each entry on the chart, and for each suggested change. If an entry or change doesn't contribute to fulfilling the vision, it doesn't go on the chart.

Prepare to deal with conflict. Carrying out any political plan will generate conflict, so it's important that you and your team are trained and ready to deal with that. Re-read the advice for dealing with conflict in Chapter Twelve. In particular, before you and your team members head out into the fray, remember that:

- you are in charge of how you respond, no matter what the provocation.
- hanging onto stereotypes and negative judgments of your opponents plays into self-fulfilling prophecies and undermines your chances of success.
- the real issues driving any conflict are rarely the ones on the table. Any conflict is like an iceberg, with seven-eighths of its mass below the water line.
- the key to success in dealing with conflict is to build trust between you and your opponent(s). And the key to building trust is to care for them.

Your whole team needs to be trained in how to deal with conflict. It's hard to build trust with opponents if others on your side think a sharp stick in the eye is the only way to go. Discuss the methods in Chapter Twelve with your team. Let team members see how the power of a caring approach works as you apply it to them.

Often it's a good idea to role-play any foreseeable conflict situations. Let your team members play themselves while you play varieties of opponents they might face. Then reverse roles. Help team members see the advantages of building trust.

■

If you want to be a good agent for change, you have to be a good teacher. Rachel Carson was one of the best. She was successful because she did her homework, she communicated well, and she cared.

Caring is key, especially if there's conflict. You've got to trade in your pride for compassion—compassion for all sentient beings, including your opponents. People are less likely to change if you attack them. Out of conflict and differences can come progress.

If you're in a conflict, keep a level head, and know your facts. I came out ahead in a public debate with the head of the Wise Use Movement not long ago because I was able to quote back to him what he'd said in the past. He couldn't wriggle out of his own history.

Young people, in particular, can be very effective in environmental politics, perhaps because they know they must live with the consequences longer than the rest of us. They need to recognize the challenges, realize that they can make a difference—and take action.

It helps, of course, if you have an organization behind you. If there's already an organization doing what you want to do, then join it. If there isn't, then start your own. I've started thirty organizations in my lifetime. One of them, Friends of the Earth, is now in fifty-seven countries.

Above all, keep up hope. Yes, many things may seem today to be going in the wrong direction, but you can help the human race do a 180-degree turn. I like this quote from Amory Lovins: "When you reach the edge of the abyss, the only progressive move you can make is to take a step back."

—David Brower, founder of Earth Island Institute

■

GETTING IT DONE

Build trust (see also page 126). Who are the individuals and groups with the most influence over the decisions that affect your issue? Which of these trust you least? Focus your trust-building efforts on these hardest targets. In Laura's case, she might start with the rural people who benefit from school funds and jobs created by clearcutting. Collectively, she has discovered, their lobbying power is enough to block any effort at logging reform.

She and the members of her team need to start the trust building by meeting with opponents in small groups or even one-on-one. Laura's first meeting should probably be with the woman who wrote such an angry letter in response to hers. Laura needs to take that woman to lunch or, better yet, sit on her porch and share a cup of tea.

The purpose of initial meetings such as these is not to repeat the same old arguments, but to start building human connections. Laura needs to make clear that she cares, not solely for the trees, but for rural schools and jobs as well. And the more she is able to show her human side—and even share her own doubts and frustrations on the issue—the easier she makes it for the other woman to respond in kind.

Needless to say, initiatives such as this work only if they are genuine. If Laura is faking it, the other woman will sense the manipulation in a moment.

Laura and this woman will never become best friends. But as each of them comes into contact with a real, personal side of the issue they hadn't known before, some trust gets established and stereotypes and other old beliefs get challenged. And as trust builds, each of them becomes more able and willing to see alternatives they could not see before. Laura follows up her visit by suggesting another meeting, this time with each of them bringing a few new contacts into the circle.

Yes, it takes courage to wade into lions' dens—and it can be incredibly effective. Your opponents will admire your courage enough to give you a hearing they might not have given you otherwise. And the sheer shock value of your move helps to undermine the complacency of the old blame game on both sides. Laura is still a long way from solving her problem, but at least she has created a link that wasn't there before.

She has also challenged her own attitudes about dealing with conflicts, the attitudes that led her to shoot from the hip when she first saw the clearcut at Big Pine. Moved by the experience of talking to the mountain woman, Laura is seeing a spillover to how she is handling other conflicts at home and at work. If she can open what appeared to be a firmly closed door on an issue as sensitive as clearcutting, she can do the same with that nasty coworker back in the city—or perhaps with her own teenager.

Probe for buried issues (see also page 125). When people who should be agreeing with you are dragging their feet instead, it's often because of underlying issues that haven't been brought to the surface. Every political issue is like an iceberg, with most of it buried below the water line, unspoken and unseen. You need to think about what the underlying issues might be for both your allies and your opponents, since these issues, and the emotions around them, may be controlling people's behaviors. Politicians may be doing what they're doing, for example, out of fear of losing votes. Bureaucrats may be hesitating because they are afraid of making waves. For nearly everyone, a key underlying issue may simply be fear of change, of leaving the security of what is known to risk doing something new.

It's hard to create lasting solutions to conflicts if buried issues such as these, and the feelings around them, are not at least acknowledged. Laura's challenge is to find ways to bring up these issues that are as non-threatening as possible. One avenue is to be open about any buried issues in herself. Her candor may encourage others to take the risk of responding in kind.

Sometimes it's possible, as a means of building trust, to find other issues or venues that are less contentious where you and your opponents can spend time together away from the issue that divides you. For example, if a local bureaucrat or politician is making life difficult for Laura's team, perhaps a team member can put himself in the same community sports program, or on the same PTA committee. Better yet, maybe somebody from Laura's team can run a rapids or hike a trail with that difficult person. Anything that lets both sides share a pleasant experience in a more relaxed atmosphere will help them build the trust they need to deal with their conflict—including the buried issues that may be fueling it.

Create a dialogue with your opponents, not a debate; use it to explore for common ground. The goal of debate is to prove yourself right. The goal of dialogue is to create enough mutual understanding and trust so that areas of shared agreement can be discovered and enlarged.

As Laura and her team begin to meet with bureaucrats, politicians, lobbyists, mill owners, and union leaders, they should do everything they can to avoid the sterile debate format of each side making statements, then jockeying for advantage. To do this, they need to demonstrate to their opponents that there are more benefits for everybody in dialogue than in debate. They should start by acknowledging those elements of the others' positions that they agree with, for example, supporting rural schools and providing rural jobs. They should also point out elements of their own proposals that might and probably should be shared by all, such as preventing disastrous spring runoffs and keeping salmon streams clear. Initial points of agreement form the basis for exploring for additional common ground.

Be street smart. No one is suggesting that, by relying on a strategy based on building trust, you give away the store. When you're playing Monopoly with your dearest friend, you still need to get control of Boardwalk and Park Place.

- Volunteer to write the first drafts of reports. The one who writes the first draft enjoys a significant advantage over the one who only gets to edit.
- Don't move the goalposts. Carefully think through what you're asking for before you ask, so that you don't have to backtrack later on. Nothing destroys trust faster than that.
- Work harder than anybody else. Doing better research, reading all the handouts instead of skimming them, really understanding a legal brief—these are the kinds of extra efforts that often pay off when the meetings are held and the final decisions made.
- Head off trouble. If, before a meeting, you're concerned about open opposition that could get out of control, try to defuse the issue in advance by meeting privately with your opponents. They may not want to cooperate, but perhaps they will want to head off a floor fight as much as you do.
- Get beyond the wiring diagrams. Knowing who reports to whom is not enough. You need to find out about as many of the unwritten pressures, linkages, and informal networks as you can. Who listens to whom? Who doesn't like whom?
- Extend your alliances. In addition to the allies you need around

the table, build and maintain connections with people in other areas tackling similar issues. You never can tell when one of them will have a breakthrough you can apply to your situation.

- Don't moralize. "How can you people destroy a forest as beautiful as . . ." is a sure way to lose someone's attention. Sure, you may be right, but moralizing makes people defensive and uncooperative.

Create a media strategy anchored to your vision. Decide what you need to say to the public, as well as why, when, and specifically to whom. Use your vision to tightly coordinate all your media efforts, including ads, flyers, speeches, letters, mass emails, a website, and interviews. Things can start moving very fast during a political campaign, and a strong vision will provide focus and consistency to your messages.

Integrate a media strategy into your overall plan. If you're succeeding with quiet negotiations, for example, you may want to forgo media entirely until you need it to gain public support for the results of your negotiations.

Avoid compromises that only postpone the conflict. As the degree of trust between you and your opponents rises, and as what you agree and disagree on becomes clearer, avoid the temptation to simply split the difference as a way of "ending" the dispute. Even if you do succeed in making such a deal, the issue will continue to fester because the basic issues have not been settled and neither side is really satisfied. Instead, now that you're so close, it's well worth a little more time and effort to try to create a solution that will last, because it's based on genuinely shared values and priorities.

It would be a mistake for Laura, for example, to agree to a deal that ruined only half the valleys and impoverished only half the schools. The impetus for conflict would remain and, like a ground fire in the forest, might seem quiet, only to burst into flames in another place. She can do better.

Create a bigger vision—one that all sides can accept. If your efforts at building trust have born some fruit, if emotions have been damped so that people are genuinely listening to each other, and if you've found at least some initial common ground, seize the moment to create a vision. Get all parties to the dispute to contribute to a picture of a solution that benefits all sides—one that doesn't just split up the existing pie, but creates a bigger pie.

Laura starts by getting permission from all the parties to use a visioning process. She explains that the purpose of the exercise is to get all sides to stop seeing the issue as *us* against *them* and to start seeing themselves as members of one community of interest, trying to solve a common problem.

She (or a third-party facilitator) then takes the group through the same kind of visioning process she used to get her own team on board. She leads everyone on a "tour" in their minds of the state's forests three years into the future. She tries to make it fun, and is careful to let her opponents share their pictures first. By the end of an hour, nearly everyone has contributed.

To many people's surprise, the pictures are remarkably compatible, even on this first run-through. Everybody sees rural schools supported, erosion and floods controlled, rural towns and livelihoods not lost, salmon runs not destroyed, the state's timber industry remaining viable, and ugly and damaging impacts on the environment minimized. The composite picture is of a future in which sound planning and fair dealing both protect the environment and meet economic and social needs. The fact that extreme views are not part of the shared vision helps further shatter stereotypes and build trust. "But I thought people like you all wanted to . . ."

Move from vision to policy. If you've taken the process this far, all parties are now ready to turn the shared vision they have just created into specific program and policy recommendations. Grappling with thorny legal and financial issues may well be part of this process, for example. If you don't reach agreement on a sensitive issue, don't let the discussion bog down there, but return to the vision, where there *is* agreement, and try to generate policy ideas by another path. Look for face-saving ways to help others climb down off earlier positions.

Ideally, the vision is now so powerful that all sides refer to it in proposing or opposing options; people start seeing their objective, not as tackling each other, but as tackling a common challenge.

Policy ideas generated by this kind of teamwork at Laura's visioning session might include, for example:

- land trades with neighboring national forests that protect key recreational and habitat land;
- subsidized experiments in selective, sustainable logging;
- a ban on clearcutting in certain areas, identified by a broad-based committee;
- state-guaranteed floors for rural school income; and
- watershed restoration, and other similar work guaranteed to maintain levels of rural employment.

A powerful visioning process creates its own momentum. People become less defensive and more creative, and they establish more connections between their individual interests and bold new policy options that serve all sides—options that could not be seen in a climate charged with suspicion or anger.

Expecting bitter wrangling, people often jump at the chance to contribute to an alternative process that clearly can produce an extremely high level of energy and creative thinking—and excellent results. Good ideas come from any quarter: environmentalists suggest options for keeping lumber mills open and mill owners design plans for stream restoration.

KEEPING IT DONE

Maintain the structure. Laura's team has gone to a lot of trouble to create a problem-solving structure that really works. They mustn't let it dissolve now that this battle is won. For one thing, they will need the structure to add the inevitable refinements to their solution over time. For another, they can use it to resolve related conflicts involving many or most of the same players.

The structure they have created is also a gift that can help their community tackle totally unrelated challenges. In creating a solution to a thorny issue that leaves all parties better off, Laura and her team have accomplished what many people would call a miracle. Now they must not erase what for their community is a uniquely effective model that can be used for solving other difficult and sensitive problems. They and all the parties to their dispute are also models themselves, capable of sharing what they did. The content of other conflicts may be different, but the human emotions and interpersonal dynamics involved are very much the same.

■

As we move into the next millennium, leadership within the national conservation arena must be measured by our commitment to include citizens from all geographic, cultural, and ethnic constituencies in our movement. We must attack head-on the reality that the United States' conservation movement is currently a homogenous group of caucasian people of wealth—that "the greening of America is white." Any perceived lack of welcome for the diversity which the conservation movement needs to embrace remains the movement's most serious barrier to success in our efforts to preserve our natural heritage.

This challenge is not only a philosophical challenge, but an economic and political challenge as well. The political power of minorities continues to grow in the U.S. to the point that, early in the next century, the long-term support needed to preserve this country's natural resources cannot be secured without the voices and votes of these partners in the American experience. If inner city and minority populations aren't encouraged to see, feel, and experience natural ecosystems from Yellowstone National Park to a local waterway or state park, they will not support legislation or other agendas to protect these lands over the compelling and competing funding needs that are closer to home.

Conservationists must develop the interest, commitment, and, ultimately, the political will among diverse constituencies to support the conservation and protection of wildlands and open space. The simple answer is that it all begins with education and opportunities to personally experience the natural world. As a community, conservation advocates must take more responsibility to fund and implement the type of educational experiences that will build this important sense of ownership.

As leaders in the conservation arena, organizations need to experiment with entirely new models of outdoor and experiential education. The Student Conservation Association (SCA), for example, recognized that its original model for bringing kids into the woods to work on conservation projects, based on the model created by the Civilian Conservation Corps, simply was not attracting minority youth. In the 1970s, we began recruiting for our programs in inner cities, but even an impactful one-time experience was not enough to truly alter perceptions of sense of place in the natural world.

In 1990, SCA began bringing our programs *into* the cities, facilitating conservation experiences for urban kids, mostly of color, which they came to see as relevant to their own lives. These programs involved teaching basic values such as land stewardship, but doing it in their urban communities as well as "in the woods." We increased the length of our commitment to these participants. By adding mentoring programs and professional internships with land management agencies, students remain actively involved for as many as six years.

Private conservation organizations, land managers, outdoor educators, and businesses serving the recreation community can make a difference by committing to creative programs and partnerships that support increasing diversity in the conservation movement. All we have to do is take leadership.

—Jay Addison Satz, Vice-President for Safety and Field Programs,
Student Conservation Association

■

Political Leadership

❑ **Successful politics is about successful leadership.** The concepts and skills needed to lead political initiatives are much the same as those needed for leading in the outdoors.

GETTING READY

❑ **Look before you leap.** Think about the obstacles, risks, conflicts, and hard work that may lie ahead. Are you ready to take them on?

❑ **Begin researching the issues,** and tapping into research that's already been done. Find out what organizations are already working on the problem you see—your best strategy may be to join them.

❑ **Form a team around a vision of the results you want.** Visions are far more powerful than facts in motivating people to action.

❑ **Find out who the decision makers are.** Where does the decision-making and decision-shaping power lie?

❑ **Make a plan.** Break your vision down into goals, and the goals into steps. Create timelines and assign responsibilities.

❑ **Prepare to deal with conflict,** using strategies aimed at building trust and exploring for common ground.

GETTING IT DONE

❑ **Build trust,** starting with those who trust you least. Start by building human connections and dispelling stereotypes.

❑ **Probe for buried issues.** It's very hard to create lasting solutions to conflicts if buried issues, and the feelings around them, aren't at least acknowledged.

❑ **Create a dialogue with your opponents, not a debate.** Use it to explore for common ground.

❑ **Be street smart.** No one is suggesting that, by relying on a strategy based on building trust, you give away the store.

❑ **Create a media strategy anchored to your vision.** Decide what you need to say to the public, as well as why, when, and specifically to whom.

❑ **Avoid compromises that only postpone the conflict.** It's well worth a little more time and effort to try to create a solution that will last.

❑ **Create a bigger vision—one that all sides can accept.** Get all parties to the dispute to contribute to a picture of a solution that benefits all sides.

❑ **Move from vision to policy**. A successful visioning process creates its own momentum, as people make more connections between their individual interests and bold new options that serve both sides.

KEEPING IT DONE

❑ **Maintain the problem-solving structure you've created**. You may need it to make refinements—and it's a model for tackling future challenges of many kinds.

For more on Political Leadership, please see *Stick Your Neck Out—A Street-Smart Guide to Creating Change in Your Community and Beyond*, also by John Graham, graham@giraffe.org.

Afterword: Expanding the Challenge

Learning to lead in the outdoors equips you for far more than leading in the outdoors. Teaching leadership, and mentoring younger leaders, is an obvious next step. Holding office within your organization is another. Getting involved in environmental issues is a third.

But there is a fourth option, and it's obvious every time you look around in your own community, or turn on the evening news. And that is the opportunity to take on leadership roles that may have nothing to do with the outdoors.

Good leadership is in short supply at every level of our lives. Your community needs good leadership to make sound decisions on land use, education, and public health and safety. The school board and the PTA where your kids go to school need good leadership to guide educational policies. Civic organizations need good leadership to work for the public good. Your business or profession needs good leadership to produce reliable products and services at fair prices, and to be a supportive neighbor in the community. And your family needs good leadership, too, especially when it's going through a rough patch.

As you learn and practice leading in the outdoors, and as you get increasingly better at it, keep these larger opportunities in mind—the skills you need are very much the same. You may have signed up to lead on the trails, but the job may turn out to be a lot bigger than you thought. Keep upping the ante. As you become more secure in meeting one type of leadership challenge, you're ready for more difficult ones.

As you broaden the scope of your leadership, don't limit yourself to strategies that are safe because they are traditional. Use and model the kind of leadership you've read about here, the kind that comes from the heart as well as the head, that stretches your imagination and your spirit, and that challenges you to balance hard-edged intellectual skills with vision, intuition, humor, and the capacity to fly by the seat of your pants. Teach and model leadership that demands that you take responsibility, not only for reaching goals, but also for your impact on peoples' lives.

THE MOUNTAINEERS, founded in 1906, is a nonprofit outdoor activity and conservation club, whose mission is "to explore, study, preserve, and enjoy the natural beauty of the outdoors. . . ." Based in Seattle, Washington, the club is now one of the largest such organizations in the United States, with seven branches throughout Washington State.

The Mountaineers sponsors both classes and year-round outdoor activities in the Pacific Northwest, which include hiking, mountain climbing, ski-touring, snowshoeing, bicycling, camping, kayaking and canoeing, nature study, sailing, and adventure travel. The club's conservation division supports environmental causes through educational activities, sponsoring legislation, and presenting informational programs. All club activities are led by skilled, experienced volunteers, who are dedicated to promoting safe and responsible enjoyment and preservation of the outdoors.

If you would like to participate in these organized outdoor activities or the club's programs, consider a membership in The Mountaineers. For information and an application, write or call The Mountaineers, Club Headquarters, 7700 Sand Point Way NE, Seattle, Washington 98115; (206) 521-6001.

The Mountaineers Books, an active, nonprofit publishing program of the club, produces guidebooks, instructional texts, historical works, natural history guides, and works on environmental conservation. All books produced by The Mountaineers Books are aimed at fulfilling the club's mission.

Send or call for our catalog of more than 500 outdoor titles:

THE MOUNTAINEERS BOOKS
1001 SW Klickitat Way, Suite 201
Seattle, WA 98134
1-800-553-4453
mbooks@mountaineersbooks.org
www.mountaineersbooks.org

About the Author

John Graham is the executive director of The Giraffe Project, an international nonprofit organization that promotes leadership and encourages people to "stick their necks out" for the common good. An outdoor enthusiast who hitch-hiked around the world at age twenty-two, he has extensive experience in hiking and climbing, including the first direct ascent of the north wall of Mount McKinley.

Following a diplomatic career during which he saw service in the revolution in Libya and the war in Vietnam, and at the United Nations, he became executive director of the Giraffe Project in 1983. In 1992, he created a series of workshops on outdoor leadership for The Mountaineers which became the basis for this book. He lives on Whidbey Island in Washington.

For more on the Giraffe Project, see www.giraffe.org

For more on John Graham's speeches, workshops and books, see www.johngrahamspeaker.org

Contact John Graham at graham@giraffe.org